tutorstack

2026 THE GAUNTLET ULTIMATE SAT®

MATH CHALLENGE

Mr. John's Test Prep + Studio Ampersand

First Edition

passthegauntlet.com

Disclaimer of Warranties and Limitation of Liability

This publication is provided for informational and educational purposes only. Tstack, LLC makes no representations, warranties, or guarantees — express or implied — regarding the accuracy, completeness, or fitness for a particular purpose of any content contained herein. No guarantee of score improvement, college admission, or academic outcome of any kind is made or implied.

Individual results will vary. Score improvement depends on a wide range of factors outside the publisher's control, including but not limited to the student's baseline ability, study habits, time invested, test anxiety, testing conditions, and prior academic preparation. The publisher expressly disclaims any responsibility for outcomes on the SAT® or any other standardized examination.

In no event shall Tstack, LLC, its officers, employees, authors, contributors, or affiliates be liable for any direct, indirect, incidental, consequential, special, or exemplary damages arising out of or in connection with your use of this publication, even if advised of the possibility of such damages. This limitation applies to all claims, whether based in contract, tort, negligence, strict liability, or any other legal theory.

By using this book, the reader acknowledges and agrees that they are doing so entirely at their own risk and that the publisher's total liability for any claim shall not exceed the purchase price of this publication.

First Printing, 2026 | ISBN: 979-8-9950707-2-6 | www.tutorstack.com

CONTENTS

THE GAUNTLET

ONLINE STUDY HUB

TAKE YOUR SCORE FURTHER

This book is just the beginning.
The full Gauntlet experience awaits.

Full-Length Tests
Adaptive, timed practice tests that mirror the real Digital SAT experience

Desmos Tips & Tricks
Detailed walkthroughs showing exactly how to use Desmos to solve SAT math faster

Elite Resources
Targeted drills, strategy guides, and score-boosting extras beyond this book

Reader Exclusive: 20% Off

Use code **GAUNTLETMATH20** — enter the ISBN found on the back cover and visit **passthegauntlet.com/redeem** to claim your discount.

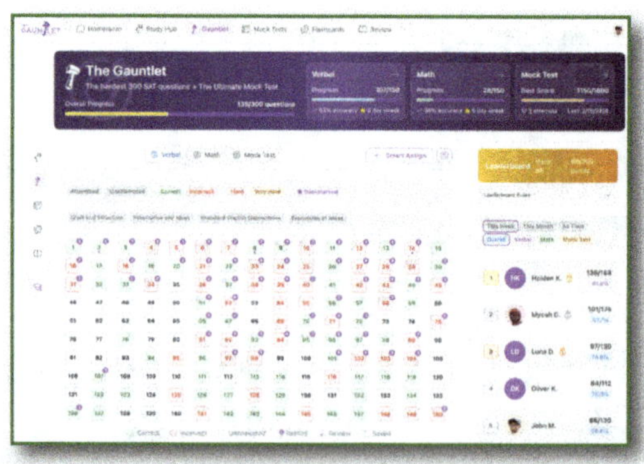

Visit us at

PASSTHEGAUNTLET.COM

Tests • Desmos Tips • Premium Resources • Community

INTRODUCTION

Welcome to The Gauntlet—the ultimate challenge for serious SAT test-takers.

This book contains 150 of the most challenging math questions you'll encounter in your SAT preparation. These aren't warm-up exercises—they're designed to push you to your limits and prepare you for the hardest content the SAT can deliver.

Why 'The Gauntlet'? In medieval times, running the gauntlet was a test of endurance and determination. Similarly, working through these 150 questions will test your algebraic fluency, problem-solving intuition, and mathematical reasoning. By the end, you'll have developed the mental toughness needed to excel on test day.

What Makes These Questions Hard?

- Multi-step problems requiring careful setup and execution
- Word problems with complex real-world scenarios
- Questions that combine multiple math concepts in a single problem
- Algebra that requires strategic manipulation rather than brute force
- Geometry and trigonometry with non-obvious solution paths
- Data analysis questions designed to test precision and interpretation

Remember: struggling with these questions is part of the learning process. Every mistake reveals a gap in your knowledge that you can now fill. Trust the process.

HOW TO USE THIS BOOK

1. **Time Yourself:** On the SAT, you have about 1:34 per Math question. Practice under timed conditions to build speed and accuracy.

2. **Attempt Before Checking:** Always solve the question yourself before reading the explanation. The struggle is where learning happens.

3. **Study Every Explanation:** Don't just check if you're right—understand WHY each step works and where common mistakes occur.

4. **Use Your Calculator Strategically:** Know when Desmos helps and when it's faster to solve by hand. Master both approaches.

5. **Track Your Progress:** Keep a log of which question types give you trouble. Focus extra practice on weak areas.

Book Structure

Questions are organized by skill type within each SAT Math domain: Algebra, Advanced Math, Problem-Solving and Data Analysis, and Geometry and Trigonometry. Answer explanations appear at the end of each section, allowing you to work through multiple questions before checking your work.

Each explanation walks you through the most efficient solution path and highlights key concepts to remember. The SAT is designed to trick you—but once you recognize these traps, you'll approach every question with confidence.

If you can identify why an answer is wrong, you're one step closer to finding why another is right.

BONUS RESOURCES

Visit **passthegauntlet.com** for video explanations and study tips
Use code **GAUNTLETMATH20** for **20% off**!

SAT MATH FORMULAS YOU MUST KNOW

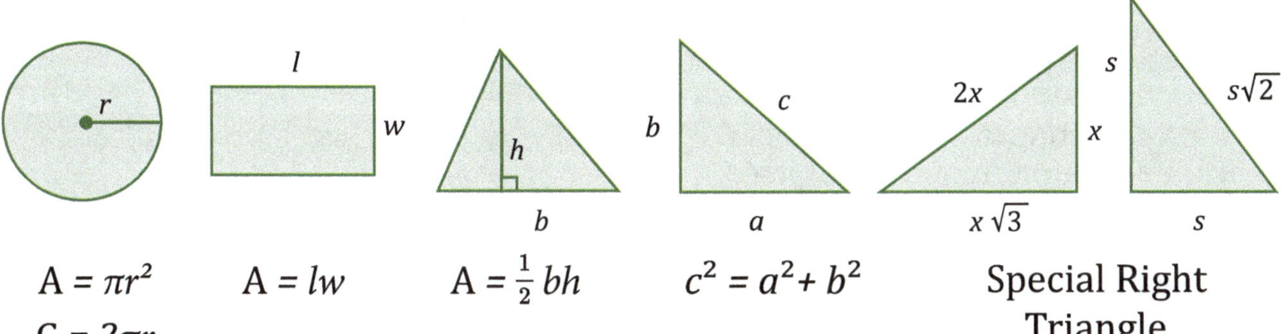

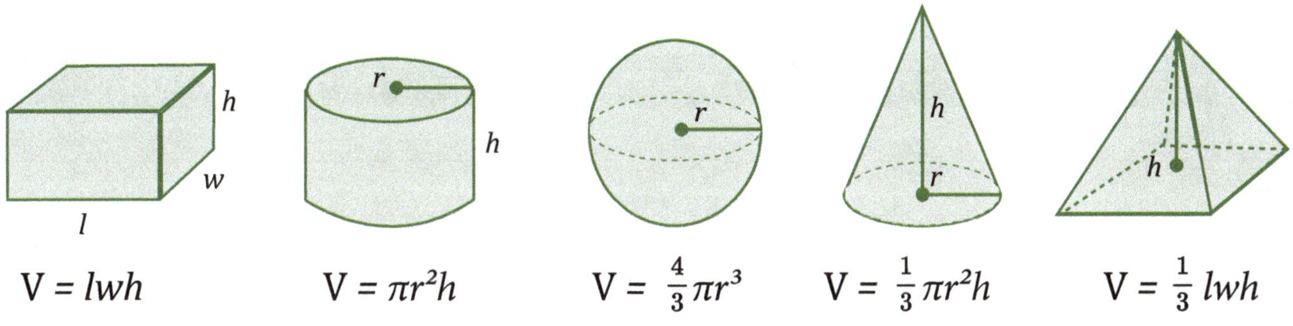

The number of degrees of arc in a circle is 360.
The number of radians of arc in a circle is 2π.
The sum of the measures in degrees of the angles of a triangle is 180

THE GAUNTLET · FLASHCARD QUIZZES

TAKE THE GAUNTLET WITH YOU.

Every formula. Every rule. Every trap. Now in your pocket.

This book gives you 150 of the hardest questions ever written for the Digital SAT®. The flashcard system on The Gauntlet gives you the foundation underneath them.

286 interactive flashcards. 37 volumes. 6 domains. Every card mirrors the structure of this book — and the structure of the test itself.

01 — WHAT'S IN THE DECK

Six domains, organized exactly like the SAT Math section, plus the strategy and reference content you won't find anywhere else:

DOMAIN	VOLUMES	CARDS
Bluebook Reference Sheet	4	21
Algebra	6	55
Advanced Math	8	75
Problem-Solving & Data Analysis	5	45
Geometry & Trigonometry	9	65
Test Strategy & Desmos	5	25

02 — HOW IT WORKS

» **Question-first format.** Every card asks before it tells. You guess, then check — exactly how the test rewards you.

» **Diagrams where the picture is the question.** Geometry and trig cards include the same kind of figure you'll see on test day.

» **Self-paced volumes.** Drill one skill at a time, or run a full domain end to end. You decide the dose.

» **Built-in spaced review.** Cards you miss come back. Cards you crush stay out of your way. Your weak spots get the attention.

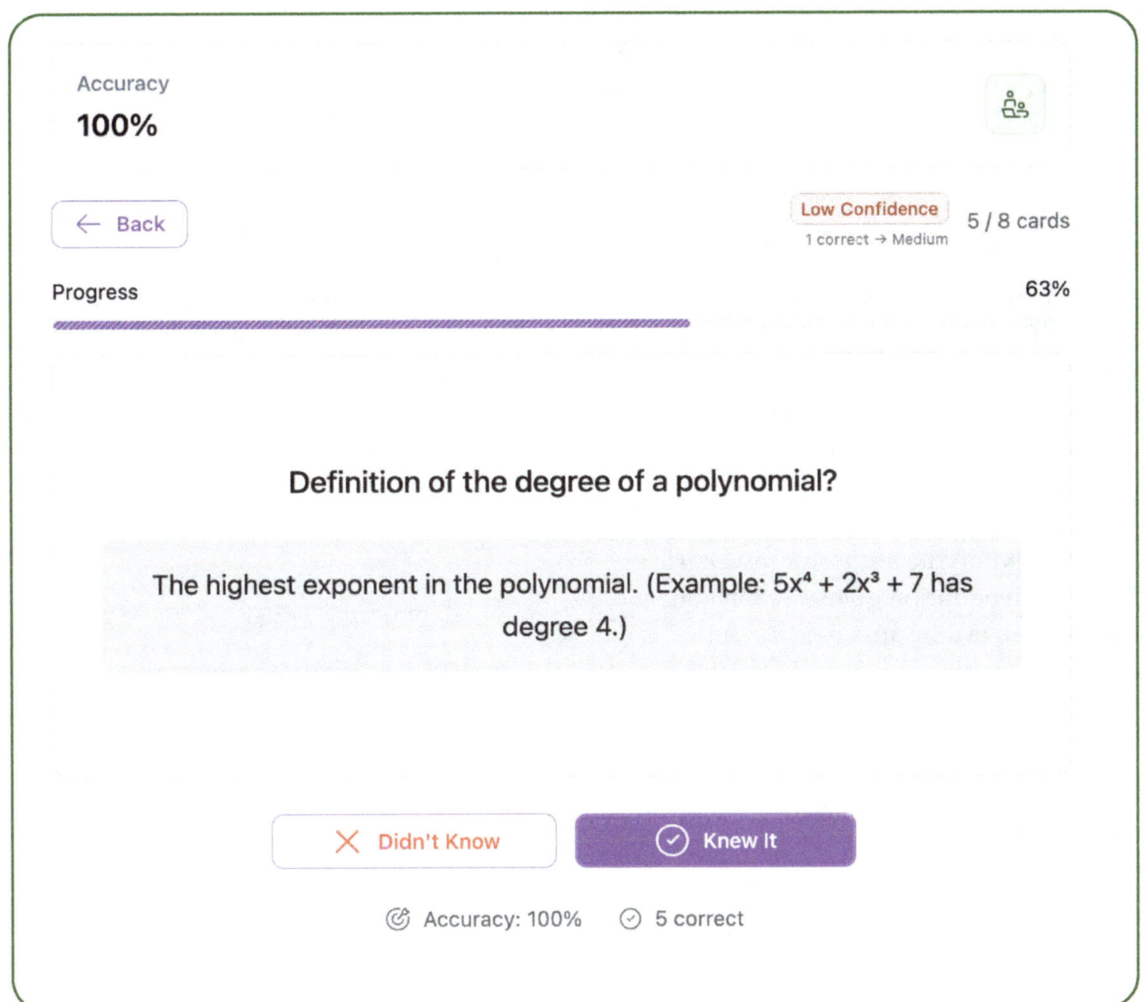

03 — WHEN TO USE THEM

Use the flashcards before you tackle each chapter to load the foundation. Use them after to lock in what you missed. Use them between sessions — on the bus, between classes, before bed — anywhere you've got 90 seconds.

The book builds the discipline. The flashcards build the recall. Together, they cover the whole test.

RUN THE GAUNTLET. CARD BY CARD.

Access the full SAT Math flashcard library at **passthegauntlet.com/sat-math-cheat-sheet**

ALGEBRA

1 LINEAR FUNCTIONS: ONE VARIABLE

During an experiment, the mean oxygen concentration in a fish tank, O(x), in milligrams per liter, increases at a constant rate in terms of the number of minutes, x, that an aerator has been running. During the test, it is observed that after 40 minutes, the concentration is 7.2 mg/l. Also, the oxygen concentration increases by 0.9 milligrams per liter when the aerator runs for 15 more minutes. Which equation gives the oxygen concentration, O(x), in milligrams per liter, in terms of the minutes, x, that the aerator has been running?

A. $O(x) = 0.06x + 7.2$

B. $O(x) = 0.06x + 4.8$

C. $O(x) = 0.9x + 7.2$

D. $O(x) = 7.2x - 288$

2 LINEAR FUNCTIONS: ONE VARIABLE

A school has three types of clubs: art, music, and science. The number of art clubs is 8 more than the number m of music clubs. The number of science clubs is twice the number of art clubs. If the school has a total of 128 clubs, which equation represents this situation?

A. $(m + 8) + m + 2(m + 8) = 128$

B. $m + (m + 8) + (2m) = 128$

C. $(m + 8) + m + (2m + 8) = 128$

D. $8m + 2m + (m + 8) = 128$

3 LINEAR FUNCTIONS: ONE VARIABLE

A car travels a total of 300 miles in two parts. On the first part it travels d miles at 40 miles per hour. On the second part it travels the remaining distance at 60 miles per hour. The total travel time is 6 hours. Which equation represents this situation?

A. $\frac{d}{60} + (\frac{300 - d}{40}) = 6$

B. $40d + 60(30 - d) = 6$

C. $\frac{300}{40} + \frac{d}{60} = 6$

D. $\frac{d}{40} + \frac{300 - d}{60} = 6$

4 LINEAR FUNCTIONS: ONE VARIABLE

A concert promoter pays a band $12,000 to perform. Tickets are sold for $80 each, but the ticketing company takes a 15% commission on the sales revenue. The promoter's profit is equal to the ticket revenue after the commission is deducted, minus the band's payment. If the promoter wants to make a profit of $9,600, which equation represents the number of tickets sold, t?

A. $(80t - 12{,}000)(1 - 0.15) = 9{,}600$

B. $(80(1 - 0.15)t - 12{,}000) = 9{,}600$

C. $(0.15)(80t) - 12{,}000 = 9{,}600$

D. $80t - (0.15)(80t) + 12{,}000 = 9{,}600$

ALGEBRA

5 LINEAR FUNCTIONS: ONE VARIABLE

$$\frac{2x+s}{r} = \frac{rx+20}{8}$$

In the given equation, s and r are constants, and s > 0. If the equation has infinitely many solutions, what is the value of s?

A. $\frac{1}{2}$

B. $\frac{3}{2}$

C. 4

D. 10

ANSWER KEY

QUESTIONS 1–5	
1	B
2	A
3	D
4	B
5	D

SOLUTIONS
LINEAR FUNCTIONS: ONE VARIABLE

Solve Variables and Expressions in Linear Equations

1. Correct Answer: B. $O(x) = 0.06x + 4.8$

The question asks for a **slope-intercept form** of a linear equation. To find the linear equation $O(x) = mx + b$, the **slope** and **y-intercept** need to be found.

The problem states that the oxygen concentration increases by 0.9 mg/l over 15 minutes. This change in concentration over time represents the **slope** of the linear function:

$$m = \frac{\Delta\ concentration}{\Delta\ time} = \frac{0.9\ mg/l}{15\ minutes} = 0.06$$

Plug this slope into the slope-intercept form:

$$O(x) = mx + b \rightarrow O(x) = 0.06x + b$$

Note: C and D can be eliminated because they do not have the correct slope.

We are given a specific point: after 40 minutes ($x = 40$), the concentration is 7.2 mg/l ($O(x) = 7.2$). Substitute these values into our equation to solve for b, the **y-intercept**:

$O(x) = 0.06x + b$	
$7.2 = 0.06(40) + b$	Plug-in (40, 7.2)
$7.2 = 2.4 + b$	Simplify
$4.8 = b$	Solve for b

Substitute $b = 4.8$ back into the linear model to evaluate the final answer:

$O(x) = 0.06x + b \rightarrow O(x) = 0.06x + 4.8$

Note: Another way to solve would be to plug-in the point (40, 7.2) into each of the given equations. This would result in only B as the equivalent statement: A) . $7.2 = 0.06(40) + 7.2 \rightarrow 7.2 \neq 9.6$; B) . $7.2 = 0.06(40) + 2.4 \rightarrow 7.2 = 7.2$; C) . $7.2 = 0.9(40) + 7.2 \rightarrow 7.2 \neq 43.2$; D) . $7.2 = 7.2(40) - 288 \rightarrow 7.2 \neq 0$.

Final expression is:

B. $O(x) = 0.06x + 4.8$

Things to remember:

- Slope-intercept form of a line is y = mx + b.
- Slope (m) measures a rate of change.
- Use the slope and a point to evaluate a y-intercept of a linear equation.

SOLUTIONS
LINEAR FUNCTIONS: ONE VARIABLE

Solve Variables and Expressions in Linear Equations

2. Correct Answer: A. $(m + 8) + m + 2(m + 8) = 128$

Start by translating the relationships into **algebraic expressions** letting m = number of music clubs:

- Number of Art Clubs → "8 more than the number m of music clubs" = $m + 8$
- Number of Science Clubs → "Twice the number of art clubs" = $2(m + 8)$

The problem states the school has a total of 128 clubs. To find the total, we add the **expressions** for all three types of clubs together:

Music Clubs + Art Clubs + Science Clubs = Total

$$m + m + 8 + 2(m + 8) = 128$$

Final expression is:

$$m + m + 8 + 2(m + 8) = 128$$

Things to remember:

- Start with identifying the variable that all terms can be written with.
- Translate keywords into operations like "more than" for addition and "total" for equals.

Solve Variables and Expressions in Linear Equations

3. Correct Answer: D. $\frac{d}{60} + \frac{300 - d}{60} = 6$

Since rate is the total distance divided by time, time can be written as a relationship between distance and rate:

$$\text{rate} = \frac{\text{distance}}{\text{time}}$$

$rate \times time = distance$ Multiply both sides by time

$time = \frac{distance}{rate}$ Divide by rate

Create an expression to describe the time spent for each part of the journey:

- First part: The car travels d miles at 40 miles per hour.

$$time = \frac{distance}{rate} \rightarrow time = \frac{d\ miles}{40\ miles\ per\ hour}$$

- Second part: The car travels 60 miles per hour for the remaining distance (300 – d).

$$\text{time} = \frac{\text{distance}}{\text{rate}} \rightarrow \text{time} = \frac{\text{300-d miles}}{\text{60 miles per hour}}$$

The problem states the total travel time is 6 hours. To find the total, we add the time from the first part to the time from the second part:

$$6\ hours = \frac{d\ miles}{40\ miles\ per\ hour} + \frac{300 - d\ miles}{60\ miles\ per\ hour}$$

Final expression is:

D. $\frac{d}{60} + \frac{300 - d}{60} = 6$

Things to remember:

- Time can be represented as distance over rate: $time = \frac{distance}{rate}$
- Total time can be calculated by adding each part of the journey

CONTINUE

Solve Variables and Expressions in Linear Equations

4. Correct Answer: B. $(80(1 - 0.15)t - 12{,}000) = 9{,}600$

To find the **equation** that represents the number of tickets sold, t, we must translate the promoter's profit structure into a linear expression: "The promoter's profit is equal to the ticket revenue after the commission is deducted, minus the band's payment." Determine the values for each of these pieces:

- Profit → The promoter wants to achieve a specific profit of $9,600.
- Ticket revenue → Tickets are sold for $80 each, represented as 80t.
- Commission → A 15% commission is taken from the sales. To represent the amount remaining after a 15% reduction, multiply ticket revenue by (1 – 0.15).
- Band's Payment → A flat fee of $12,000.

Create an **equation** where profit equals ticket revenue minus the commission and band's payment:

profit = ticket revenue – commission – band's payment

$$9600 = 80(1 - 0.15)t - 12000$$

Final expression is:

B. $(80(1 - 0.15)t - 12{,}000) = 9{,}600$

Things to remember:

- When a percentage is deducted, multiply by the remaining percentage.
- Follow order of operations when writing and solving expressions.

5. Correct Answer: D. 10

For a linear equation to have **infinitely many solutions**, both sides of the equation must be mathematically identical. This means once the equation is simplified, the coefficients of x must be equal, and the constant terms must be equal. Simplify the equation by first cross-multiplying:

$$\frac{2x + s}{r} = \frac{rx + 20}{8}$$

$8(2x + s) = r(rx + 20)$	Cross-multiply
$16x + 8s = r^2 x + 20r$	Distribute

Because there are **infinitely many solutions**, the x-term on the left must equal the x-term on the right, and the constant on the left must equal the constant on the right. Solve for r using the x coefficients:

$16x = r^2x$	
$16 = r^2$	Divide by x
$4 = r$	Take the square root

Solve for s using the constant terms:

$8s = 20r$	
$8s = 20(4)$	Plug-in $r = 4$
$8s = 80$	Simplify
$s = 10$	Divide by 8

Therefore, the value of s is:

D. 10

Things to remember:

- An equation has infinitely many solutions only if the two sides represent the same linear expression.
- When dealing with proportions, cross-multiply to simplify and solve.

CONTINUE

ALGEBRA

6 LINEAR FUNCTIONS: ONE VARIABLE

A nutrition bar company modeled the weekly sales S (in units) as a linear function of the selling price p (in dollars). The company sold 18,400 units when the price was $3.20 per bar and 14,800 units when the price was $4.40 per bar. Based on this model, what is the weekly sales S when the price is $3.95 per bar?

7 LINEAR FUNCTIONS: ONE VARIABLE

A science museum allows groups to borrow virtual reality headsets for a project. A group can borrow up to 6 headsets. The first headset requires 5 minutes to calibrate, and each additional headset requires 2 minutes to calibrate. If it takes t minutes to calibrate n headsets (where n is a positive integer and $n \leq 6$), which of the following equations gives t in terms of n?

A. $t = 2n + 3$

B. $t = 5n - 2$

C. $t = 2n + 5$

D. $t = 2n + 7$

8 LINEAR FUNCTIONS: ONE VARIABLE

The table below shows three values of x and their corresponding values of h(x), where $h(x) = f(x) + (-4)$ and f is a linear function.

x	h(x)
-2	-3
4	5
10	13

Based on this information, what is the y-coordinate of the y-intercept of the graph of $y = f(x)$ in the xy–plane?

9 LINEAR FUNCTIONS: ONE VARIABLE

A storage tank initially contains 120 liters of water. The target is 600 liters. A pump fills the tank at 9 liters per minute for the first 20 minutes after it is turned on, and then at 15 liters per minute until the target is reached. According to this model, at the end of t minutes after the pump is turned on, where $t > 20$, which of the following functions gives the predicted number of liters still needed to reach the target?

A. $R(t) = 600 - 15t$

B. $R(t) = 480 - 15t$

C. $R(t) = 600 - 9t$

D. $R(t) = 300 - 15(t + 20)$

10 LINEAR FUNCTIONS: ONE VARIABLE

A community center charges \$200 for the first class a participant takes and \$120 for each additional class. Each participant pays this amount individually for the classes they attend. Let $C(s, p)$ represent the total cost, in dollars, for s classes taken by p participants, where s and p are positive integers. Which of the following functions correctly represents $C(s, p)$?

A. $C(s, p) = 120sp + 200$

B. $C(s, p) = 200sp + 120$

C. $C(s, p) = 120sp + 80p$

D. $C(s, p) = 200 + 120s + p$

11 LINEAR FUNCTIONS: ONE VARIABLE

$$C(x) = 1.35(x - 42.75) + 18.6$$

The function C gives the cost, in dollars, of producing a part when x kilograms of material are used. If the material amount increases by 4.20 kilograms, by approximately how much does the cost increase, in dollars?

A. 4.20

B. 5.67

C. 18.6

D. 23.1

ANSWER KEY

QUESTIONS 6-11	
6	16150
7	A
8	11/3
9	A
10	C
11	B

Don't just check the answer—master the method.
Get specific Desmos tips for each solution online. Gain access to The Gauntlet Mock Test and track your progress in real-time at **passthegauntlet.com.** Use code **GAUNTLETMATH20** to unlock 20% off your digital dashboard.

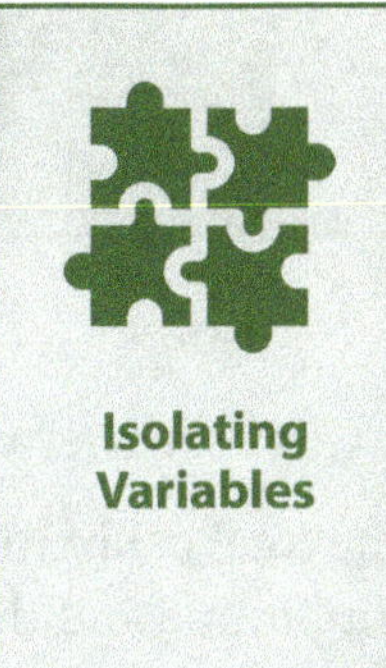

6. Correct Answer: 16150

To find the weekly sales S when the price is \$3.95, we first need to establish the **linear relationship** between price (p) and sales (S) using the provided data points.

The **slope** (m) represents the change in units sold for every dollar increase in price. We use the two points from the problem (3.20, 18400) and (4.40, 14800):

$$m = \frac{y^2 - y^1}{x^2 - x^1} \rightarrow \frac{14800 - 18400}{4.40 - 3.20}$$

$$m = \frac{-3600}{1.20} = -3000$$

Using the linear model S = $mp + b$, we substitute one of the points and the slope to solve for b:

$S = mp + b$	
$S = -3000p + b$	Substitute $m = -3000$
$18400 = -3000(4.40) + b$	Plug-in (4.40, 14800)
$18400 = -9600 + b$	Simplify
$28000 = b$	Add 9600 to both sides

Note: Either given point (3.20, 18400) or (4.40, 14800) could have been plugged in to solve for b.

The final model can be expressed as S=-3000p+28000. Now, substitute in p = 3.95 to evaluate the weekly sales when the price is \$3.95:

$S = -3000p + 28000$	
$S = -3000(3.95) + 28000$	Plug-in $p = 3.95$
$S = -11850 + 28000$	Multiply
$S = 16150$	Simplify

The weekly sales equals:

16150

Things to remember:

- Slope-intercept form of a line is $y = mx + b$.
- Use the slope and a point to evaluate a y-intercept of a linear equation.

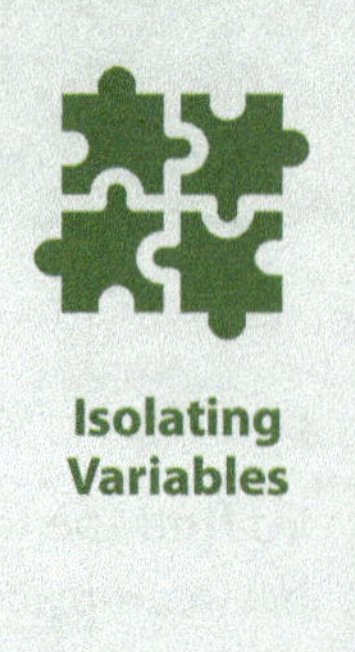

7. Correct Answer: A. $t = 2n + 3$

The total calibration time t in terms of the number of headsets n is found by identifying the fixed initial time and the constant rate for additional units:

- The first headset takes 5 minutes → + 5
- Each additional headset takes 2 minutes → $2(n - 1)$

The total time t is the sum of the initial calibration and the recurring calibration for all remaining headsets. Create an equation using this model:

$$t = 5 + 2(n - 1)$$

Simplify the expression to determine which answer matches:

$$t = 5 + 2(n - 1)$$

$t = 5 + 2n - 2$	Distribute
$t = 2n + 3$	Combine Like Terms

The final equation is:

A. $t = 2n + 3$

Things to remember:

- When a rate applies only after the first item, use $n - 1$ to avoid double-counting the first unit.
- Sometimes expressions need to be simplified to find a matching answer.

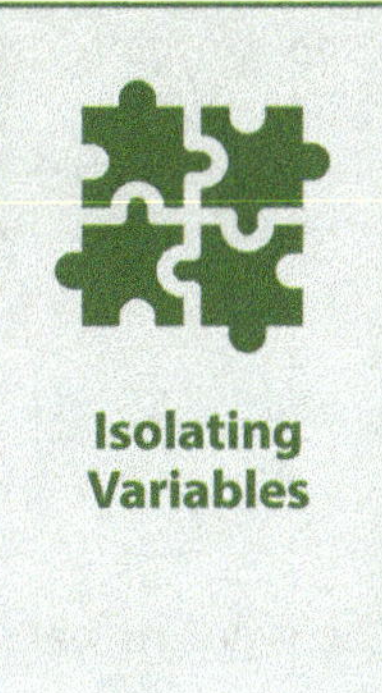

8. Correct Answer: $\frac{11}{3}$

The question asks for the y-coordinate of the **y-intercept** of the graph of $y = f(x)$. The y-intercept of any function occurs when $x = 0$. Therefore, the goal is to find the value of $f(0)$.

The problem provides the relationship $h(x) = f(x) + (x - 4)$. To isolate $f(x)$, subtract $(x - 4)$ from both sides of the equation: $f(x) = h(x) - (x - 4)$

Next, use the values from the table to find at least two points that lie on the graph of $f(x)$:

For $x = -2$, the table shows $h(-2) = -3$. So plug these values into $f(x)$:

- $f(x) = h(x) - (x - 4)$
- $f(-2) = -3 - (-2 - 4)$
- $f(-2) = -3 - (-6)$
- $f(-2) = -3 + 6$
- $f(-2) = 3$

This gives the point (–2, 3).

For $x = 4$, the table shows $h(4) = 5$. So plug these values into $f(x)$:

- $f(x) = h(x) - (x - 4)$
- $f(4) = 5 - (4 - 4)$
- $f(4) = 5 - 0$
- $f(4) = 5$

This gives the point (4, 5).

Since $f(x)$ is a linear function, use these two points to find the slope (m):

$$m = \frac{y_2 - y_1}{x_2 - x_1}$$

$$m = \frac{5 - 3}{(4 - (-2))}$$

$$m = \frac{2}{6} = \frac{1}{3}$$

Now, use the **slope-intercept form** ($y = mx + b$) and the point (4, 5) to solve for the y-intercept (b):

$5 = \frac{1}{3}(4) + b$	Plug-in (4, 5)
$5 = \frac{4}{3} + b$	Multiply by 4
$b = 5 - \frac{4}{3}$	Subtract

$b = \frac{15}{3} - \frac{4}{3} = \frac{11}{3}$ Simplify

The y-coordinate of the y-intercept of $f(x)$ is $\frac{11}{3}$.

Things to Remember:

- The y-intercept of a function is the value of y when $x = 0$.
- For any linear function, the slope (m) is the constant rate of change between any two points on the line.
- You can manipulate function notation equations just like standard algebraic equations to isolate a specific variable or function.

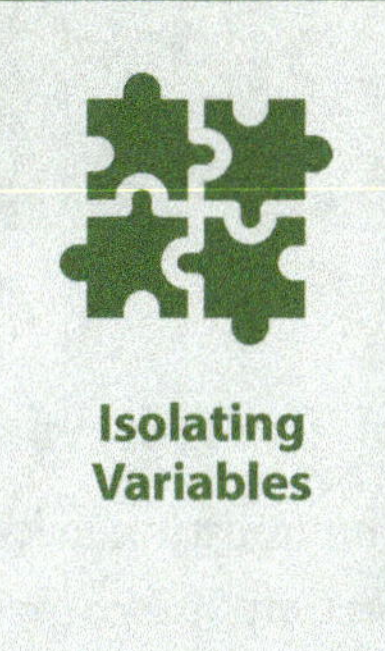

9. Correct Answer: A. $R(t) = 600 - 15t$

The question asks for a function R(t) that calculates the number of liters still needed to reach a target of 600 liters when $t > 20$. To find this, we must first determine how much water is already in the tank at time t.

First, account for the amount of water in the tank after the first stage (0 – 20 minutes):

- Starting volume at $t = 0$: 120 liters
- Volume added in the first 20 minutes:

$$9\ \frac{liters}{minute} \times 20 \text{ minutes} = 180 \text{ liters}$$

- Total volume at $t = 20$:

$$120 + 180 = 300 \text{ liters}$$

Next, determine the volume added during the second stage ($t > 20$). For any time t greater than 20, the pump has been running at the new rate for $(t - 20)$ minutes.

Additional volume added after 20 minutes:

$15(t - 20)$ liters

Now, combine these to find the total volume $V(t)$ in the tank at any time $t > 20$:

$V(t) = 300 + 15(t - 20)$	Total volume at $t = 20$ plus additional volume
$V(t) = 300 + 15t - 300$	Distribute 15
$V(t) = 15t$	Simplify

Finally, the liters still needed, $R(t)$, is the difference between the target (600 liters) and the current volume $V(t)$:

$$R(t) = 600 - V(t)$$

$$R(t) = 600 - 15t$$

Things to Remember:

- When a rate changes at a specific time, calculate the "state of the system" (the total amount accumulated) at that exact moment to use as a new starting point.
- Make sure to follow through with the entire question to ensure you are solving for the correct final answer.

SOLUTIONS
LINEAR FUNCTIONS: ONE VARIABLE

10. Correct Answer: C. $C(s, p) = 120sp + 80p$

The question asks for a function $C(s, p)$ representing the total cost for s classes taken by p participants. Since each participant pays this amount individually, the first step is to determine the cost for a single person and then multiply that total by the number of participants.

First, determine the cost for one participant taking s classes:

- The first class costs 200 dollars.
- Each additional class costs 120 dollars. If a person takes s classes, the number of "additional" classes is $(s - 1)$.
- Cost for one person = $200 + 120(s - 1)$

Next, simplify the expression for one participant:

$C(s) = 200 + 120s - 120$	Distribute
$C(s) = 120s + 80$	Simplify

Finally, since there are p participants and each is charged this same amount individually, multiply the single-person cost by p to find the total function $C(s, p)$:

$C(s, p) = p(120s + 80)$	Multiply by p
$C(s, p) = 120sp + 80p$	Distribute

This matches choice C.

Things to Remember:

- When dealing with "first item" vs "additional items," the number of additional items is always the total quantity minus one $(n - 1)$.
- Total cost for multiple independent groups or individuals is found by calculating the cost of one unit and multiplying by the total number of units (p).

 ·

11. Correct Answer: B. 5.67

The equation $C(x) = 1.35(x - 42.75) + 18.6$ is a **linear function**. In a **linear function**, the rate of change is represented by the **slope**. Simplify the expression to determine the value of the slope:

$C(x) = 1.35(x - 42.75) + 18.6$

$C(x) = 1.35x - 57.7125 + 18.6$ Distribute

$C(x) = 1.35x - 76.3125$ Simplify

The slope is the value in front of the variable. In the simplified form, this is 1.35:

$$y = mx + b$$

$$C(x) = 1.35x - 76.3125$$

To find the total increase in cost for a specific increase in material, multiply the rate of change by the amount of the increase:

- Rate of change (slope): 1.35 dollars per kilogram
- Increase in material: 4.20 kilograms
- Total cost increase: $1.35 \times 4.20 = 5.67$

Therefore, an increase of 4.20 kilograms results in a cost increase of approximately 5.67 dollars.

Note: Alternative Approach → You can also solve this by picking any two values for x that have a difference of 4.20 and calculating the difference in their resulting C(x) values. For example, if you choose x = 42.75, the cost is 18.6. If you increase x by 4.20 to 46.95, the new cost is 1.35(4.20) + 18.6, which is 5.67 + 18.6 = 24.27. The difference (increase) is 24.27 – 18.6 = 5.67.

Things to Remember:

- In a linear function, the slope (m) represents a constant rate of change.
- When a question asks for a "change" or "increase" based on another change in a linear model, you only need to focus on the slope, as the constant terms do not affect the rate of increase.
- The total change in the dependent variable (y) is equal to the slope (m) times the change in the independent variable (x).

12 LINEAR FUNCTIONS : TWO VARIABLES

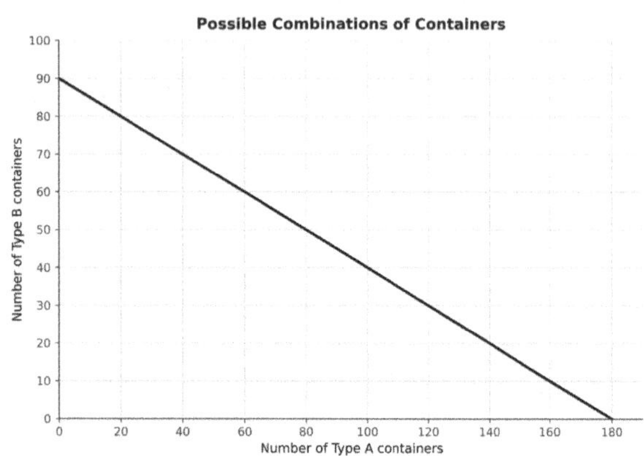

A shipping company uses two types of cargo containers: Type A and Type B. Each container of the same type has the same weight. The total combined weight of all containers is 162,000 kilograms. The graph shows the possible combinations of the number of Type A containers, x, and the number of Type B containers, y, that the company could use. Based on the graph, which of the following is closest to the weight, in kilograms, of each Type A container?

A. 600

B. 700

C. 900

D. 1800

13 LINEAR FUNCTIONS : TWO VARIABLES

Two lines, r and s, are perpendicular. The points $(3, n)$ and $(9, n + 4)$ lie on line r. The lines intersect at the point $(9, n + 4)$.

Which of the following points could lie on line s?

A. $(n + 6, 28)$

B. $(15, n + 2)$

C. $(11, n + 1)$

D. $(21, n - 8)$

14 LINEAR FUNCTIONS : TWO VARIABLES

A construction project requires exactly 150 pounds of material to be delivered. The delivery can be made using two types of carts. Each Type P cart carries 60 pounds for every 2 carts used. Each Type F cart carries 100 pounds for every 3 carts used. The project manager may use any combination of the two cart types. Let p be the number of Type P carts and f be the number of Type F carts. Which equation represents all possible values of p and f that result in exactly 150 pounds being delivered?

A. $\frac{2}{60}\ p + \frac{3}{100}\ f = 150$

B. $\frac{60}{2}\ p + \frac{100}{3}\ f = 150$

C. $\frac{2}{60}\ (150) = p + f$

D. $\frac{2}{60}\ (150) + \frac{3}{100}\ (150) = p + f$

15 LINEAR FUNCTIONS : TWO VARIABLES

The table gives the coordinates of two points on a line in the xy-plane.

x	y
t	2
t+5	4

The line intersects the point $(t - 2, p)$, where t and p are constants. What is the value of p?

16 LINEAR FUNCTIONS : TWO VARIABLES

x	y
2	m
r	8
10	14

The table above represents a linear equation with a slope of $\frac{3}{2}$. What is the value of $m + r$?

A. 8

B. 10

C. 12

D. 14

ANSWER KEY

QUESTIONS 12-16	
12	C
13	C
14	B
15	6/5
16	A

ANSWER KEY

QUESTIONS 12-16	
12	C
13	C
14	B
15	6/5
16	A

Points on a Line with Unknown Coordinates

12. Correct Answer: C. 900

First, interpret the meaning of the graph's axes and intercepts:

- The x-**axis** represents the number of Type A containers used.
- The **y-axis** represents the number of Type B containers used.

The **x-intercept** of the graph is located at (180, 0). This specific point represents a scenario where the company uses 180 Type A containers and 0 Type B containers to reach the total weight.

Next, use the total combined weight provided in the problem to find the weight of a single Type A container:

Type A + Type B = Total Weight

$180A + 0B = 162{,}000$	Substitute in x-intercept
$180A = 162{,}000$	Remove B variable
$A = \frac{160{,}000}{180}$	Divide
$A = 900$	

The weight of each Type A container is 900 kilograms.

Things to Remember:

- On a graph showing combinations of two items, the intercepts represent "all of one and none of the other".
- To find the unit weight or value from an intercept, divide the total value by the number of units shown at that intercept.

CONTINUE

Points on a Line with Unknown Coordinates

13. Correct Answer: C. (11, $n + 1$)

This question involves finding the equation for line r to determine the equation for line s. Start by finding the **slope** of line r using the two given points, (3, n) and (9, $n + 4$):

$$m = \frac{(y_2 - y_1)}{(x_2 - x_1)}$$

$$m = \frac{(n + 4) - n}{9 - 3}$$

$$m = \frac{4}{6} = \frac{2}{3}$$

Since line s is perpendicular to line r, their slopes are negative reciprocals. The **negative reciprocal** of $\frac{2}{3}$ is $-\frac{3}{2}$. Use this slope and the point (9, $n + 4$), to find the equation for line s in **point-slope** form.

$$y - y_1 = m(x - x_1)$$
$$y - (n + 4) = -\frac{3}{2}(x - 9)$$

Test the points in the choices to see which one satisfies the equation for line s. To test Choice C, (11, $n + 1$), substitute $x = 11$ into the equation to determine if $y = n + 1$:

$$y - (n + 4) = -\frac{3}{2}(11 - 9)$$

$y - (n + 4) = -\frac{33}{2} + \frac{27}{2}$	Distribute
$y - (n + 4) = -3$	Simplify
$y = (n + 4) - 3$	Add
$y = n + 1$	Simplify

Since the result matches the y-coordinate in Choice C, this point must lie on line s.

Things to Remember:

- Perpendicular lines have slopes that are negative reciprocals of each other.
- Use point – slope form when given a slope and a point on a line.

14. Correct Answer: B. $\frac{60}{2}p + \frac{100}{3}f = 150$

The question asks for an equation that represents the possible combinations of Type P and Type F carts needed to deliver exactly 150 pounds of material. To solve, the weight capacity per single cart for each type needs to be determined.

First, calculate the rate of weight per cart for each type:

Type P:

- 2 carts carry 60 pounds
- Weight per cart = $\frac{60 \text{ pounds}}{2 \text{ carts}}$

Type F:

- 3 carts carry 100 pounds
- Weight per cart = $\frac{100 \text{ pounds}}{3 \text{ carts}}$

Next, set up the total weight equation using p to represent the number of Type P carts and f to represent the number of Type F carts.

- The total weight contributed by Type P carts is $\frac{60}{2}p$.
- The total weight contributed by Type F carts is $\frac{100}{3}f$.

The sum of these weights must equal the project requirement of exactly 150 pounds:

$$\frac{60}{2}p + \frac{100}{3}f = 150.$$

This expression matches Choice B.

Things to Remember:

- When given a rate, calculate the unit rate for each variable to build a linear equation.
- Do not simplify the fractions if the answer choices leave them in their original rate form.

Points on a Line with Unknown Coordinates

15. Correct Answer: $\frac{6}{5}$

To solve for the **y-coordinate** of the point $(t - 2, p)$, first determine the **slope** of the line and then use its equation to find the missing coordinate.

First, calculate the **slope** (m) of the line using the two points provided in the table, $(t, 2)$ and $(t + 5, 4)$:

$$m = \frac{(y_2 - y_1)}{(x_2 - x_1)}$$

$$m = \frac{(4 - 2)}{(t + 5 - t)}$$

$$m = \frac{2}{5}$$

Next, establish the equation of the line. Using the **point-slope form** of a linear equation with the point $(t, 2)$ and the slope $\frac{2}{5}$:

$$y - y_1 = m(x - x_1)$$

$$y - 2 = \frac{2}{5}(x - t)$$

Finally, substitute the coordinates of the target point $(t - 2, p)$ into the equation to solve for p:

$y - 2 = \frac{2}{5}(x - t)$	
$p - 2 = \frac{2}{5}((t - 2) - t)$	Plug-in point
$p - 2 = \frac{2}{5}(-2)$	Simplify
$p - 2 = -\frac{4}{5}$	Multiply
$p = \frac{6}{5}$	Add

The value of p is $\frac{6}{5}$.

Things to Remember:

- To find a missing coordinate on a line, substitute the known coordinate into the line's equation and solve for the unknown.

Points on a Line with Unknown Coordinates

16. Correct Answer: A. 8

To solve for $m + r$, each constant can be found by using the **slope**. In a **linear equation**, every point is equal distance from each other and should create the same slope with any other point.

First, find the value of m using the points (2, m) and (10, 14) and the given slope of $\frac{3}{2}$:

$$\text{slope} = \frac{(y_2 - y_1)}{(x_2 - x_1}$$

$$\frac{3}{2} = \frac{(14 - m)}{(10 - 2)}$$

$$3(10 - 2) = 2(14 - m)$$

$$3(8) = 28 - 2m$$

$$24 = 28 - 2m$$

$$-4 = -2m$$

$$m = 2$$

Next, find the value of r using the points (r, 8) and (10, 14) and the given slope of $\frac{3}{2}$:

$$\text{slope} = \frac{(y_2 - y_1)}{(x_2 - x_1)}$$

$$\frac{3}{2} = \frac{(14 - 8)}{(10 - r)}$$

$$3(10 - r) = 2(14 - 8)$$

$$30 - 3r = 2(6)$$

$$30 - 3r = 12$$

$$-3r = -18$$

$$r = 6$$

Finally, compute the sum of m and r:

$$m + r = 2 + 6 = 8$$

This matches Choice A.

Things to Remember:

- The slope of a linear function is constant between any two points on its graph.
- Always double-check your final answer against the specific request in the question—in this case, the sum $m + r$, rather than just the individual values.

CONTINUE

ALGEBRA

17 SYSTEMS OF LINEAR EQUATIONS

$$5x + 7y = 19$$

$$15x + 21y = 57$$

For each real number t, which of the following points lies on the graph of each equation in the xy-plane for the given system?

A. $(r, \frac{19 - r}{7})$

B. $(\frac{19 - r}{5}, r)$

C. $(\frac{21r}{15}, r)$

D. $(10 - r, r)$

18 SYSTEMS OF LINEAR EQUATIONS

$$12x + 23y = 41$$

$$x + 7y = 10$$

The solution to the given system of equations is $(x, y) = (\frac{p}{61}, \frac{w}{61})$, where p and w are integers. What is the value of p?

19 SYSTEMS OF LINEAR EQUATIONS

$$27(x - m) = 27y + 81m$$

One equation in a system of two linear equations is given where m is a positive constant. The system has no solution. Which equation could be the second equation in this system?

A. $9x - 9y = -45m$

B. $9x + 9y = 15m$

C. $9x - 3y = -63m$

D. $9x + 9y = -21m$

20 SYSTEMS OF LINEAR EQUATIONS

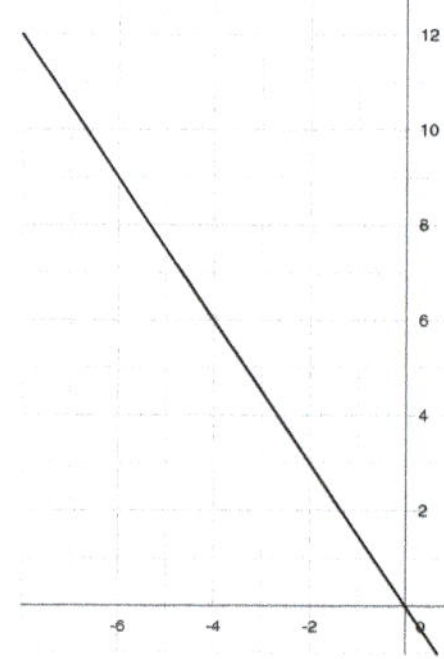

The graph of line h is shown in the xy–plane. Line k is defined by $210x + py = w$, where p and w are constants. If line k is graphed in this xy–plane, resulting in a system of two linear equations with infinitely many solutions, what is the value of $p + w$?

ALGEBRA

21 SYSTEMS OF LINEAR EQUATIONS

$$3x + ky = 150$$

$$-2x + ky = -30$$

In the given system of equations, k is a constant. In the xy–plane, the graphs of these equations intersect at the point $(p, 14)$, where p is a constant. What is the value of k?

A. 2

B. 3

C. 14

D. 26

22 SYSTEMS OF LINEAR EQUATIONS

One of the equations in a system of two linear equations is given as $15x - 21y = 105$. The second equation is written in the form $25x - 35y = t$, where t is a constant. If the system has no solution, which of the following is NOT a possible value of t?

A. 35

B. 105

C. 135

D. 175

23 SYSTEMS OF LINEAR EQUATIONS

$$\frac{y}{5} + 4(x - 6) = 50$$

$$\frac{y}{2} - 4(x - 6) = 20$$

The solution to the given system of equations is (x, y). What is the value of $15y$?

A. 100

B. 1000

C. 1250

D. 1500

24 SYSTEMS OF LINEAR EQUATIONS

One equation in a system of linear equations is $\frac{x}{4} - \frac{y}{6} = 5$. The system has no solution. Which of the following could be the other equation?

A. $3x - 2y = 60$

B. $3x - 2y = 84$

C. $6x - 4y = 120$

D. $9x - 6y = 180$

ALGEBRA

25 SYSTEMS OF LINEAR EQUATIONS

$$\frac{2}{5}x + \frac{1}{2}y = \frac{5}{6}y + 2$$

$$\frac{m}{3}x - \frac{5}{6}y = 18$$

In the given system of equations, m is a constant. If the system has no solution, what is the value of m?

26 SYSTEMS OF LINEAR EQUATIONS

$$(p - q) - 8(r + s) = 400$$

$$(p - q) + 4(r + s) = 640$$

For the given system of equations, what is the value of $5(p - q)$?

A. 2400

B. 2600

C. 2800

D. 3000

27 SYSTEMS OF LINEAR EQUATIONS

A factory produces two types of widgets: Type A and Type B. Each Type A widget requires 3 units of metal and 2 units of plastic. Each Type B widget requires 5 units of metal and 4 units of plastic. In one week, the factory used 390 units of metal and 280 units of plastic to produce these widgets. How many Type B widgets were produced?

A. 30

B. 50

C. 70

D. 80

SEE SOLUTIONS ON NEXT PAGE

CONTINUE

ANSWER KEY

QUESTIONS 17-27	
17	B
18	57
19	A
20	150
21	B
22	D
23	D
24	B
25	3
26	C
27	A

Systems with One Solution

17. Correct Answer: B. $\left(\frac{19 - 7r}{5}, r\right)$

The question asks for a point that lies on the graph of both equations in the system for any real number r. To find this, examine the relationship between the two equations in the system to determine that the second equation is exactly three times the first equation:

$$3(5x + 7y = 19) \rightarrow 15x + 21y = 57$$

Since the equations are multiples of each other, they represent the same line in the xy-plane, meaning any point that satisfies one equation will satisfy the other.

Next, find the general form of a point on this line by solving for one variable in terms of the other. Rearrange the first equation to isolate x:

$5x + 7y = 19$

$5x = 19 - 7y$ Subtract

$x = \frac{19 - 7y}{5}$ Divide

Since the answers are in terms of r, substitute y = r into the expression to solve:

$$y = r \rightarrow x = \frac{19 - 7r}{5}$$

The point in the form (x, y) is therefore $\left(\frac{19 - 7r}{5}, r\right)$. This matches Choice B.

Things to Remember:

- If one equation in a system is a multiple of the other, the system has infinitely many solutions because the equations represent the same line.
- To find a general point (x, y) on a line given a parameter r, solve the equation for one variable and substitute r for the other.

CONTINUE

18. Correct Answer: 57

To solve for p in the **solution** to the **system of equations**, use **substitution** to evaluate x and y. First, express x in terms of y in the second equation:

$$x + 7y = 10$$

$$x = 10 - 7y$$

Next, substitute this expression for x into the first equation to solve for y:

$$12(10 - 7y) + 23y = 41$$

$$120 - 84y + 23y = 41$$

$$120 - 61y = 41$$

$$-61y = -79$$

$$y = \frac{79}{61}$$

Now, solve for x by substituting the value of y back into the earlier expression:

$$x = 10 - 7(\frac{79}{61})$$

$$x = \frac{610}{61} - \frac{553}{61}$$

$$x = \frac{57}{61}$$

Finally, match the calculated value of x with the given form $\frac{p}{61}$:

$$\frac{p}{61} = \frac{57}{61}$$

$$p = 57$$

Things to Remember:

- The substitution method is often the most direct way to solve a system when one variable has a coefficient of 1.
- Carefully manage signs and distribution when substituting expressions into linear equations

Systems with No Solution

19. Correct Answer: A. $9x - 9y = -45m$

A **system of two linear equations** has **no solution** when the two lines are **parallel** but not identical. This means they must have the same **slope** but different **y–intercepts.**

To identify the parallel line from the answer choices, the given equation should be rearranged into **standard form** ($Ax + By = C$):

$$27(x - m) = 27y + 81m$$

$$27x - 27m = 27y + 81m$$

$$27x - 27y = 81m + 27m$$

$$27x - 27y = 108m$$

Next, look at the answer choices. Most of them begin with "9x," so scale the simplified equation down by dividing every term by 3:

$$(27x - 27y = 108m) \div 3 \rightarrow 9x - 9y = 36m$$

For a system to have no solution, the second equation must have the same **coefficients** for x and y (the same left-hand side) but a different **constant** (the right-hand side):

Comparing this to the choices matches Choice A:

$$9x - 9y = -45m$$

This has the correct left-hand side and a different constant since m is a positive constant. This line is **parallel** to the original and will result in **no solution**.

Things to Remember:

- Parallel lines have the same slope but different y-intercepts, resulting in no solution for the system.
- If both sides of two equations are identical or multiples of each other, they represent the same line and have infinitely many solutions.

20. Correct Answer: 150

For line h and line k form a system with **infinitely many solutions** they must be **identical.** To solve for line k, the equation for line h can first be determined from its graph.

The line passes through the origin (0, 0) and the point (–5, 7). Calculate the **slope** (m) first using these points.

$$m = \frac{(y_2 - y_1)}{(x_2 - x_1)}$$

$$m = \frac{(7 - 0)}{(-5 - 0)}$$

$$m = -\frac{7}{5}$$

Since the y–intercept is 0, the equation in **slope–intercept form** is:

$$y = mx + b \rightarrow y = -\frac{7}{5}x$$

Next, convert the equation of line h into standard form ($Ax + By = C$) to match the format of line k:

$$y = -\frac{7}{5}x$$

$5y = -7x$	Multiply by 5
$7x + 5y = 0$	Add $7x$

Finally, scale this equation to match the x–coefficient of 210 given for line k:

$$30(7x + 5y = 0) \rightarrow 210x + 150y = 0$$

Matching this to the equation gives a value of 150 for p and 0 for w. Use this to calculate The value of $p + w$:

$$p + w = 150 + 0 = 150$$

Things to Remember:

- A system has infinitely many solutions if the two equations represent the same line.
- When a line passes through the origin (0, 0), its y–intercept is 0, and its equation simplifies to the form $y = mx$.

21. Correct Answer: B. 3

Since the point (p, 14) is the intersection of the two given equations, it must satisfy both equations in the system. **Substituting** $y = 14$ into both equations allows for solving for the unknown constants:

$$3x + 14k = 150$$

$$-2x + 14k = -30$$

Next, use the elimination method to solve for x. Subtract Equation 2 from Equation 1 to eliminate the variable k:

$(3x + 14k) - (-2x + 14k) = 150 - (-30)$	Subtract
$3x + 2x + 14k - 14k = 150 + 30$	Distribute
$5x = 180$	Simplify
$x = 36$	Divide

This makes the point of intersection (36, 14), so substitute $x = 36$ and $y = 14$ back into either of the equations to solve for k. Using Equation 1:

$3(36) + 14k = 150$	Plug-in (36, 14)
$108 + 14k = 150$	Multiply
$14k = 42$	Subtract
$k = 3$	Divide

The value of k is 3, which matches Choice B.

Things to Remember:

- An intersection point (x, y) of two lines satisfies both equations in a system.
- The elimination method is effective when equations share a common term, allowing you to subtract one equation from the other to isolate a single variable.

Systems with No Solution

22. Correct Answer: D. 175

The question asks for the value that is NOT a possible value for t given that the system of linear equations has no solution. A system has **no solution** when the two lines are **parallel** but not identical, meaning they have the same slope but different y–intercepts.

To determine which value will not work for t, both equations need to be simplified. First, simplify the first equation:

$$15x - 21y = 105$$

$5x - 7y = 35$ Divide by 3

Next, simplify the second equation:

$$25x - 35y = t$$

$5x - 7y = \frac{t}{5}$ Divide by 5

Now, compare the two simplified equations. Both have the same left–hand side, which means they already have the same slope. For the system to have **no solution,** the constants on the right–hand side must be different:

$$35 \neq \frac{t}{5}$$

For the system to have **infinitely many solutions,** the constants must be equal. Solve for the value of t that makes the lines identical:

$$35 = \frac{t}{5}$$
$$175 = t$$

If $t = 175$, the two equations represent the same line and the system has **infinitely many solutions.** Therefore, 175 is the only value that does not result in a system with **no solution.**

Things to Remember:

- A system of linear equations has no solution if the lines are parallel (same slope) but have different y–intercepts.
- A system has infinitely many solutions if the equations represent the same line, meaning they have the same slope and same y–intercept.

23. Correct Answer: D. 1500

The question asks for the value of $15y$ based on the solution (x, y) to a given system of linear equations. Because one term, $4(x - 6)$, appears as a positive in the first equation and a negative in the second, the elimination method is the most efficient approach.

First, add the two equations together to eliminate the x-terms:

$$\left[\frac{y}{5} + 4(x - 6) = 50\right] + \left[\frac{y}{2} - 4(x - 6) = 20\right]$$

$$\frac{y}{5} + \frac{y}{2} = 70$$

Next, solve for y by finding a common denominator for the fractions on the left-hand side:

$\frac{y}{5} + \frac{y}{2} = 70$	
$\frac{2y}{10} + \frac{5y}{10} = 70$	Find common denominator
$\frac{7y}{10} = 70$	Add
$7y = 700$	Multiply
$y = 100$	Divide

Finally, calculate the value requested in the question, which is $15y$:

$$15y = 15 \times 100 = 1500$$

This matches Choice D.

Things to Remember:

- To add fractions with different denominators, always find the least common multiple (LCM) to create a common denominator.
- Always read the final part of the question carefully to ensure you are providing the specific value requested.

CONTINUE

SOLUTIONS
SYSTEMS OF LINEAR EQUATIONS

24. Correct Answer: B $3x - 2y = 84$

For a system of linear equations to have **no solutio**n, the two lines must be **parallel**, meaning they have the same **slope** but different **y–intercepts**.

Clear the fractions of the given equation to make it more easily comparable to the answer choices:

$$12(\frac{x}{4} - \frac{y}{6} = 5) \rightarrow 3x - 2y = 60$$

Now we can compare our simplified equation to the answer choices:

A. $3x - 2y = 60$: This is the exact same equation. A system with two identical equations has infinitely many solutions because the lines are on top of each other.

B. $3x - 2y = 84$: The left-hand side is identical ($3x - 2y$), which means the lines have the same slope. However, the constant on the right is different (84 vs 60). This means the lines are parallel and will never intersect, resulting in no solution.

C. $6x - 4y = 120$: If the equation is divided by 2 it becomes $3x - 2y = 60$. This is the same line as the original, resulting in infinitely many solutions.

D. $9x - 6y = 180$: If the equation is divided by 3 it becomes $3x - 2y = 60$. This also represents the same line.

Because choice B has the same **coefficients** for x and y but a different **constant**, it is the correct choice.

Things to Remember:

- No solution means the lines are parallel → they have the same slope but different y-intercepts.
- In the form $Ax + By = C$, if the A and B values are the same (or proportional) but the C values are different, the system has no solution.

SOLUTIONS
SYSTEMS OF LINEAR EQUATIONS

25. Correct Answer: 3

For a system of two **linear equations** to have **no solution**, the lines must be **parallel** but have different **y-intercepts**. This means that when the equations are written in **standard form** ($Ax + By = C$), the **coefficients** of x and y must be **proportional**, while the constants on the right side are not.

To solve for m, simplify both equations and compare their slopes. First, simplify the first equation by moving all y terms to the left side and clearing the fractions:

$\frac{2}{5}x + \frac{1}{2}y = \frac{5}{6}y + 2$

$\frac{2}{5}x - \frac{1}{3}y = 2$	Subtract
$6x - 5y = 30$	Multiply by 15

Next, clear the fractions in the second equation by multiplying by the least common denominator, 6:

$$6(\frac{m}{3}x - \frac{5}{6}y = 18) \rightarrow 2mx - 5y = 108$$

For the system to have **no solution**, the left-hand sides of these two simplified equations must be identical while the right-hand sides remain different. Compare the two resulting left-hand sides of the equations to solve for m:

$6x - 5y = 2mx - 5y$	Set left-sides equal
$6x = 2mx$	Cancel out y
$6 = 2m$	Cancel out x
$3 = m$	Divide by 2

Things to Remember:

- No solution occurs when lines have the same slope but different y-intercepts (parallel lines).
- Clearing fractions and writing both equations in $Ax + By = C$ form makes it easy to compare the ratios of the coefficients.

26. Correct Answer: C. 2800

When dealing with **a system of equations** that presents more than two **variables**, simplify the equations by rewriting in terms of only two variables. Let $x = (p - q)$ and $y = (r + s)$. Now, rewrite the system using x and y:

$$(p - q) - 8(r + s) = 400 \rightarrow x - 8y = 400$$

$$(p - q) + 4(r + s) = 640 \rightarrow x + 4y = 640$$

To solve for x, use the **elimination method** by subtracting the two equations:

$(x - 8y = 400) - (x + 4y = 640)$	Subtract
$-12y = 240$	Eliminate x
$y = 20$	Divide

Now, substitute y = 20 back into one of the equations to solve for x:

$x - 8(20) = 400$	Substitute y
$x - 160 = 400$	Multiply
$x = 560$	Add

Since we defined x as $(p - q)$, $(p - q) = 560$. The question asks for $5(p - q)$:

$$5 \times 560 = 2800$$

Therefore, Choice C is the best answer.

Things to Remember:

- When you see the same expression repeated in a system, replace it with a single variable to simplify the algebra.
- Adding or subtracting equations is often the fastest way to isolate a variable in a linear system.

Systems with One Solution

27. Correct Answer: A. 30

This word problem requires translating verbal descriptions into a **system of linear equations.** To do this, first define the variables:

- Let a = the number of Type A widgets produced.
- Let b = the number of Type B widgets produced.

Next, create an equation for each resource used:

- Metal Equation:
  - Type A uses 3 units and Type B uses 5 units for a total of 390 units
  - $3a + 5b = 390$
- Plastic Equation:
  - Type A uses 2 units and Type B uses 4 units for a total of 280 units
  - $2a + 4b = 280$

To find the number of Type B widgets (b), use the **substitution** method by first simplifying the plastic equation and isolating the variable a:

$$(2a + 4b = 280) \div 2 \rightarrow a + 2b = 140$$

$$a = 140 - 2b$$

Now, substitute this expression for a into the metal equation to solve for b:

$3(140 - 2b) + 5b = 390$	Substitute
$420 - 6b + 5b = 390$	Distribute
$420 - b = 390$	Simplify
$b = 30$	Subtract

The factory produced 30 Type B widgets.

Things to Remember:

- Assign a variable to each unknown quantity mentioned in the question.
- Check if any equation can be divided by a common factor to make the numbers easier to work with before solving.

ALGEBRA

28 LINEAR INEQUALITIES

A caterer charges $25 per guest for the first 80 guests. For each guest beyond 80, the charge is $32 per guest. What is the least number of guests needed so the total bill is at least $2,400?

A. 92

B. 93

C. 94

D. 100

29 LINEAR INEQUALITIES

To ship packages, Company A charges a flat fee of $12 plus $4.20 per kilogram of weight. Company B charges a flat fee of $8 plus $5.00 per kilogram of weight. If x represents the number of kilograms of a package, for what values of x will Company B's shipping cost be greater than Company A's shipping cost?

A. $x \leq 2$

B. $x \geq 4$

C. $x > 5$

D. $x < 3$

30 LINEAR INEQUALITIES

In a set of four consecutive even integers, ordered from least to greatest, the first integer is represented by x. The sum of the second and fourth even integers is at least 30 more than twice the first even integer. Which inequality represents this situation?

A. $(x + 2) + (x + 4) \leq 2x + 30$

B. $(x + 2) + (x + 6) \geq 2x + 30$

C. $(x + 2) + (x + 4) \geq 2x + 30$

D. $(x + 2) + (x + 6) \geq x + 30$

SEE SOLUTIONS ON NEXT PAGE

CONTINUE

ANSWER KEY

QUESTIONS 28-30	
28	B
29	C
30	B

Don't just check the answer—master the method.
Get specific Desmos tips for each solution online. Gain access to The Gauntlet Mock Test and track your progress in real-time at **passthegauntlet.com.** Use code **GAUNTLETMATH20** to unlock 20% off your digital dashboard.

Solving Linear Inequalities

28. Correct Answer: B. 93

The question asks for the least number of guests needed for the total bill to be at least \$2,400. To solve this, break the total cost into two parts based on the pricing structure.

First, calculate the cost for the first 80 guests based on the idea that the caterer charges \$25 per guest for the first 80 people:

$$80 \text{ guests} \times \$25/\text{guest} = \$2{,}000$$

Since the target total bill is \$2,400 and the first 80 guests only cover \$2,000, determine how much more money must be generated by additional guests:

$$\$2{,}400 - \$2{,}000 = \$400$$

Let x represent the number of guests beyond the initial 80. These guests are charged \$32 each. This additional charge needs to be at least \$400:

$$32x \geq 400$$

$$x \geq \frac{400}{32}$$

$$x \geq 12.5$$

The total number of guests is the initial 80 plus the additional x guests:

$$\text{Total guests} \geq 80 + 12.5$$

$$\text{Total guests} \geq 92.5$$

Because the number of guests must be a whole number, and 92 guests would result in a bill slightly less than \$2,400, round up to the next whole person. Therefore, the least number of guests needed is 93.

Things to Remember:

- "At least" means greater than or equal to (≥), while "more than" would mean strictly greater than (>).
- In real-world word problems check if your final answer must be a whole number. Always check if you need to round up or down based on the context of "least" or "greatest."

SOLUTIONS
LINEAR INEQUALITIES

29. Correct Answer: C. $x > 5$

The objective is to find the range of weight, represented by x, for which Company B's shipping cost exceeds Company A's shipping cost. This requires creating two linear expressions and comparing them using an **inequality**.

First, identify the components of each company's price based on the flat fee and the rate per kilogram.

- Company A: \$12 fee plus \$4.20 per kg → $12 + 4.2x$
- Company B: \$8 fee plus \$5.00 per kg → $8 + 5x$

The problem asks for the values of x where Company B's cost is greater than Company A's cost. Set-up the inequality and then solve for x:

$8 + 5x > 12 + 4.2x$	Set-up inequality
$0.8x + 8 > 12$	Combine x values
$0.8x > 4$	Subtract 8
$x > 5$	Divide

Therefore, $x > 5$, represents the number of kilograms of a package when Company B's shipping cost is greater than Company A's shipping cost.

Things to Remember:

- Pay close attention to wording; "greater than" translates to >, while "at least" or "no less than" translates to ≥.
- When solving inequalities, the steps are identical to solving equations, with one major exception: you must flip the inequality sign if you multiply or divide both sides by a negative number.

30. Correct Answer: B. $(x + 2) + (x + 6) \geq 2x + 30$

To translate the given information into an equation, define each part of the set and then apply the specific conditions described.

The problem states there are four consecutive even integers, starting with x. Consecutive even integers always differ by 2. Therefore, the set is defined as:

- First integer: x
- Second integer: $x + 2$
- Third integer: $x + 4$
- Fourth integer: $x + 6$

Now, break down the specific relationship described in the text.

"The sum of the second and fourth even integers" → $(x + 2) + (x + 6)$

"30 more than twice the first even integer" → $2x + 30$

Putting these pieces together results in:

$$(x + 2) + (x + 6) \geq 2x + 30$$

This matches choice B.

Things to Remember:

- For consecutive integers, use x, $x + 1$, $x + 2$... For consecutive even or odd integers, use x, $x + 2$, $x + 4$... because both even and odd numbers skip by 2.
- Keywords like "at least" (>=) and "no more than" (<=) are essential for picking the correct inequality sign.

ADVANCED MATH

31 NONLINEAR FUNCTIONS

$$f(x) = \frac{3}{8}x - \frac{5}{6}$$
$$k(x) = 4x + \frac{7}{3}$$

The functions f and k are defined by the equations shown. Which expression is equivalent to $f(t) \cdot$ k(t)?

A. $\frac{3}{2}t^2 - \frac{59}{24}t - \frac{35}{18}$

B. $\frac{3}{2}t^2 + \frac{59}{24}4t - \frac{35}{18}$

C. $\frac{3}{2}t^2 + \frac{7}{8}t + \frac{35}{18}$

D. $\frac{3}{2}t^2 - \frac{7}{8}t - \frac{35}{18}$

32 NONLINEAR FUNCTIONS

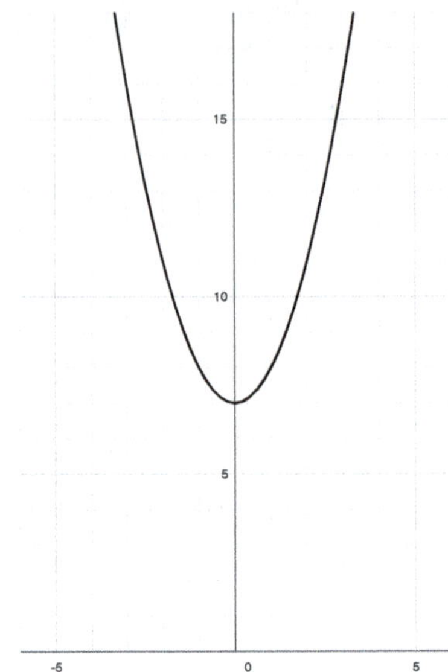

The graph of $y = g(x) + 6$ is shown, where $g(x) = ax^2 + bx + c$ and a, b, c are constant. For how many values of x does $g(x) = 0$?

A. Three

B. Two

C. One

D. Zero

ADVANCED MATH

33 NONLINEAR FUNCTIONS

x	y
0	32
5	42
10	32

The table above shows the relationship between the variables x and y. Which quadratic equation represents this relationship?

A. $y = x^2 - 14x + 32$

B. $y = -\frac{1}{2}x^2 + 5x + 32$

C. $y = -\frac{2}{5}x^2 + 4x + 32$

D. $y = -\frac{2}{5}x^2 - 10x + 32$

34 NONLINEAR FUNCTIONS

The quadratic function g is defined by $g(x) = px^2 + qx + r$, where p, q, and r are constants. The graph of $y = g(x)$ in the xy-plane has zeros at $x = -4$ and $x = 6$. If p is an integer greater than 1, which of the following could be the value of $p + q$?

A. –5

B. –1

C. 3

D. 5

35 NONLINEAR FUNCTIONS

A quadratic function h is defined by $h(x) = p(x - k)^2 - 10$, where p and k are constants. The graph of $y = h(x)$ passes through the points (0, 35) and (4, 10). If $0 < k < 4$, what is the value of k?

36 NONLINEAR FUNCTIONS

The functions m, n, and k are defined below, where $x \geq 0$. Which of the following equations displays, as a constant or coefficient, the minimum value of the function it defines, where $x \geq 0$?

I. $m(x) = 25(1.2)^{x+4}$

II. $n(x) = 10(1.5)(0.8)^{x+2}$

III. $k(x) = 12(1.15)^x$

A. III only

B. I and II only

C. II and III only

D. I, II, and III

ADVANCED MATH

37 NONLINEAR FUNCTIONS

A warehouse has 600 kilograms of a certain chemical in storage. Due to natural evaporation, every 4 hours the amount of chemical remaining decreases by 15 percent compared to the amount 4 hours earlier. Which function gives the amount of chemical remaining after x hours, where x is a multiple of 4?

A. $f(x) = 600(0.15)^{\frac{x}{4}}$

B. $f(x) = 600(0.85)^{4x}$

C. $f(x) = 600(0.85)^{\frac{x}{4}}$

D. $f(x) = 600(0.15)^{4x}$

38 NONLINEAR FUNCTIONS

Which of the following expressions has a factor of $x + 3b$, where b is a positive integer constant?

A. $5x^2 + 28x + 30b$

B. $5x^2 + 40x + 30b$

C. $5x^2 + 34x + 30b$

D. $5x^2 + 52x + 30b$

39 NONLINEAR FUNCTIONS

If $(x + \frac{1}{2})^2 - \frac{9}{4} = 0$, what is a possible value of $(x - \frac{5}{2})^2$?

A. $\frac{1}{4}$

B. $\frac{9}{4}$

C. $\frac{25}{4}$

D. $\frac{49}{4}$

40 NONLINEAR FUNCTIONS

A container of soup is set on a counter. The temperature in kelvins t minutes after it is set down is modeled by the function $T(t) = 300 + (415 - 300)(2.718)^{-0.12t}$. According to this function, what was the approximate temperature of the soup, in kelvins, when it was set on the counter?

A. 250

B. 271

C. 300

D. 415

ADVANCED MATH

41 NONLINEAR FUNCTIONS

One solution to $2x^2 - 16x - 656 = 0$ can be written as $x = h \pm \sqrt{k}$, where h and k are integers. What is the value of $h + k$?

A. 344

B. 348

C. 360

D. 388

42 NONLINEAR FUNCTIONS

The function g is defined by $g(x) = a^x + b$, where a and b are constants and $a > 0$. In the xy–plane, the graph of $y = g(x)$ has a y–intercept at (0, –11) and passes through the point (2, 52). What is the value of $a - b$?

43 NONLINEAR FUNCTIONS

The function $P(t) = 350(\frac{49}{50})^{t-6} + 12$ gives the estimated number of items in a warehouse, where t is the number of months since tracking began. After how many months was the number of items estimated to be 362?

44 NONLINEAR FUNCTIONS

The function f is defined by $f(x) = a\sqrt{(b - x)}$, where a and b are constants. In the xy-plane, the graph passes through the point (18, 0), and $f(-2) < 0$. Which of the following must be true?

A. $a > 0$

B. $b < 0$

C. $b < a$

D. $b > a$

ADVANCED MATH

45 NONLINEAR FUNCTIONS

In the equation $\sqrt{(5x + k)} = x + 3$, k is an integer constant. If the equation has no real solutions, what is the greatest possible value of k?

46 NONLINEAR FUNCTIONS

The function E models the energy stored in a battery pack, in watt-hours, t years after 2015 and is given by $E(t) = 500(1.02)^{\frac{t}{3}}$. According to the model, the stored energy is predicted to increase by 2 percent every m months. What is the value of m?

A. 3

B. 12

C. 24

D. 36

47 NONLINEAR FUNCTIONS

A satellite's battery capacity degrades over time. The function $C(t) = 400(0.5)^{\frac{t}{20}}$ gives the capacity, in watt-hours, of a 400 - Wh battery t years after the satellite begins operation. Which of the following best describes the meaning of $C(4 \cdot 20) = 25$?

A. The capacity is approximately 25 watt - hours 4 years after it begins operation.

B. The capacity is approximately 25 watt - hours 4 half-life periods (80 years) after it begins operation.

C. The capacity is approximately 4 watt - hours 20 years after it begins operation.

D. The capacity is approximately 20 watt - hours 25 years after it begins operation.

48 NONLINEAR FUNCTIONS

A streamer's weekly audience is modeled by an exponential function $A(t) = a \cdot b^t$, where a and b are positive constants and t is the number of weeks since the channel launch. The graph of $y = A(t)$ passes through the points (0, 11) and (2, 539). What is the value of ab?

A. 22

B. 49

C. 77

D. 539

ADVANCED MATH

49 NONLINEAR FUNCTIONS

The function f is defined by $f(x) = k(1.5)^x$, where k is a constant. The value of $f(x)$ increases by 50% for every increase of x by 1. For which of the following functions, where k is a constant, does the value of $g(x)$ increase by 50% for every increase of x by 3?

A. $g(x) = f(x + 3)$

B. $g(x) = f(3x)$

C. $g(x) = f(\frac{x}{3})$

D. $g(x) = f(x)+3$

50 NONLINEAR FUNCTIONS

Which of the following expressions has a factor of $x + 3k$, where k is a positive integer constant?

A. $3x^3 + 12x^2 + 18kx$

B. $4x^3 + 18x^2 + 18kx$

C. $5x^3 + 21x^2 + 27kx$

D. $6x^3 + 30x^2 + 18kx$

51 NONLINEAR FUNCTIONS

A backup system starts with 250 copies of a file. Due to automated replication, the number of copies triples every 45 minutes after deployment. Which equation gives N, the number of copies, t minutes after deployment?

A. $N = 250(3)^{\frac{t}{45}}$

B. $N = 250(45)^{3t}$

C. $N = 250(t + 45)^3$

D. $N = 250 + \frac{3t}{45}$

52 NONLINEAR FUNCTIONS

The function g is a quadratic function. Its graph has a vertex at (–2, 7) and passes through the point (0, 31). If $f(x) = g(x + 3)$, what is the value of $f(3) - f(1)$?

A. 84

B. 112

C. 144

D. 168

ADVANCED MATH

53 NONLINEAR FUNCTIONS

In the equation $\sqrt{(m-2x)}=x-10$, m is a real constant. The equation has exactly one real solution. What is the minimum possible value of $3m$?

54 NONLINEAR FUNCTIONS

A parabola opens upward and has x–intercepts at –3 and 9. Its equation has the form $f(x) = ax^2 + bx + c$, where a, b, and c are constants and $0 < a \leq 2$. If a is an integer, which of the following could be the y–intercept of the parabola?

A. –45

B. –54

C. –72

D. –90

55 NONLINEAR FUNCTIONS

What is the sum of all real solutions to the equation $\frac{(x-6)(x+1)(x-3)}{(x-3)(x-8)}=0$?

A. 3

B. 5

C. 6

D. 8

56 NONLINEAR FUNCTIONS

Which expression is a factor of $12x^2(x+20) - 12(x+20)^2$?

A. $x - 4$

B. $x + 4$

C. $12x - 5$

D. $12x + 20$

57 NONLINEAR FUNCTIONS

x	y
-3	5
7	0
11	$\frac{8}{3}$

The table shows values of x and their corresponding values of $f(x)$, where $f(x)= \frac{kx - 28}{x - 5}$ and k is a constant. What is the value of k?

58 NONLINEAR FUNCTIONS

A video platform's concurrent viewers P(m) (in thousands) m minutes after a stream starts is modeled by $P(m) = 80 \cdot S^{\frac{m}{3}}$, where $S > 1$ and is a constant. The predicted concurrency increases by p percent every 180 seconds. What is p in terms of S?

A. $100(S - 1)$

B. $100(S^{60} + 1)$

C. $100(S^{60} - 1)$

D. $100(S^{\frac{1}{3}} - 1)$

59 NONLINEAR FUNCTIONS

A quadratic function models the height h, in feet, of a projectile above the ground t seconds after launch. The projectile was launched from a height of 25 feet and reached its maximum height of 625 feet 5 seconds after it was launched. Based on the model, what was the height, in feet, of the projectile 2 seconds after it was launched?

60 NONLINEAR FUNCTIONS

The function p is defined by $p(x) = k((x - 2)^2 - m)((x - 2)^2 - n)$, where k, m, and n are constants. In the xy–plane, the graph of $y = p(x)$ passes through the points (1, 50) and (6, 500). What is the value of $p(-2) + p(6)$?

CONTINUE

ANSWER KEY

QUESTIONS 31-60			
31	A	46	D
32	C	47	B
33	C	48	C
34	A	49	C
35	12/5	50	B
36	A	51	A
37	C	52	D
38	B	53	60
39	B	54	B
40	D	55	B
41	B	56	B
42	20	57	4
43	6	58	A
44	D	59	409
45	8	60	1000

Composite Functions

31. Correct Answer: A. $\frac{3}{2}t^2 - \frac{59}{24}t - \frac{35}{18}$

The question asks for the product of two functions, $f(t)$ and $k(t)$. This requires substituting t for x in the given equations and then multiplying the resulting binomials.

Replace the variable x with t in both function definitions:

$$f(x) = \frac{3}{8}x - \frac{5}{6} \rightarrow f(t) = \frac{3}{8}t - \frac{5}{6}$$

$$k(x) = 4x + \frac{7}{3} \rightarrow k(t) = 4t + \frac{7}{3}$$

To find $f(t) \cdot k(t)$, multiply the two binomials:

$(\frac{3}{8}t - \frac{5}{6}) \times (4t + \frac{7}{3})$

$\frac{3}{2}t^2 + \frac{7}{8}t - \frac{10}{3}t - \frac{35}{18}$ FOIL

$\frac{3}{2}t^2 - \frac{59}{24}t - \frac{35}{18}$ Simplify

Things to Remember:

- When a function is given as $f(x)$ but you are asked for $f(t)$, simply replace every instance of x with t.
- When multiplying two binomials, ensure you distribute all four pairings: First, Outer, Inner, and Last.
- To add or subtract terms with different denominators, you must find a common denominator.

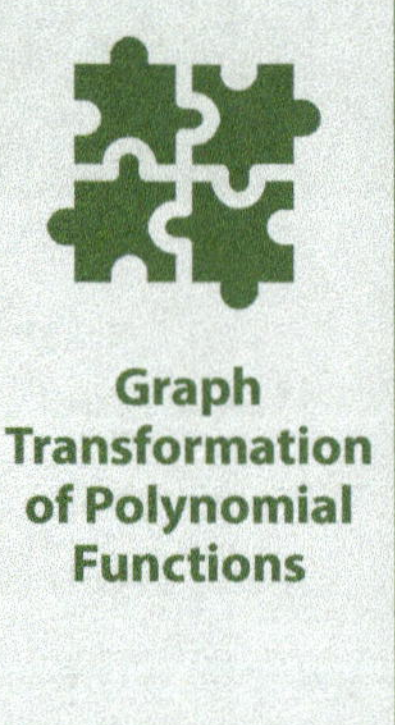

32. Correct Answer: C. One

The question asks for the number of values of x for which $g(x) = 0$, which is equivalent to finding the number of **x–intercepts** of the function $g(x)$.

The graph shown represents the function $g(x) + 6$. Since this graph is $g(x) + 6$, it has been shifted up 6 units from the original function $g(x)$.

To find the graph of $g(x)$, we must perform the inverse transformation by shifting the given graph down 6 units. If the vertex at (0, 6) is moved down 6 units, the new vertex for $g(x)$ will be at (0, 0).

Since the vertex of $g(x)$ is (0, 0), there is exactly one value of x (which is $x = 0$) where the function equals zero.

Therefore, $g(x) = 0$ for exactly one value of x.

Things to Remember:

- Adding a constant k to a function $(f(x) + k)$ shifts the entire graph up k units, while subtracting k shifts it down.
- The solutions to $g(x) = 0$ are the x–coordinates where the graph crosses or touches the x–axis.
- If the vertex of a parabola lies on the x–axis, the quadratic has exactly one real root (a "double root"). If the vertex is above the x–axis and opens upward, it has zero real roots.

33. Correct Answer: C. $y = -\frac{2}{5}x^2 + 4x + 32$

The table shows a symmetric quadratic relationship where (5, 42) is the midpoint between (0, 32) and (10, 32). This means that the vertex of the parabola is at (5, 42). Use this point and **vertex form** of a quadratic equation to construct the initial framework of the **quadratic.**

$$y = a(x - h)^2 + k \rightarrow y = a(x - 5)^2 + 42$$

To solve for a, substitute in (0, 32) and simplify:

$$32 = a(0 - 5)^2 + 42$$

$$32 = a(5)^2 + 42$$

$$32 = 25a + 42$$

$$-10 = 25a$$

$$a = -\frac{10}{25} = -\frac{2}{5}$$

Substitute a into the original equation and then expand to match one of the answers:

$$y = -\frac{2}{5}(x - 5)^2 + 42$$

$y = -\frac{2}{5}(x^2 - 10x + 25) + 42$ Expand

$y = -\frac{2}{5}x^2 + 4x - 10 + 42$ Distribute

$y = -\frac{2}{5}x^2 + 4x + 32$ Simplify

Things to Remember:

- Look for x and y–intercepts in tables as good starting points for constructing equations.
- Using two different points (other than the y–intercept) will always provide enough information to solve for the missing a and b coefficients in quadratics.

34. Correct Answer: A. –5

The problem states that the graph has **zeros** at $x = -4$ and $x = 6$. The **quadratic** function with these zeros can be written in **factored form** as:

$$g(x) = p(x + 4)(x - 6)$$

Expand the factored form to find the **standard form** of the equation:

$g(x) = p(x + 4)(x - 6)$	
$g(x) = p(x^2 + 4x - 6x - 24)$	FOIL
$g(x) = px^2 + 4px - 6px - 24p$	Distribute
$g(x) = px^2 - 2px - 24p$	Simplify

Compare the expanded form to the given equation to compare terms:

$$g(x) = px^2 + - 2px - 24p \rightarrow g(x) = px^2 + qx + r$$

Use the given relationship to evaluate q:

$-2px = qx$

$-2p = q$ Cancel x

The question asks for the value of $p + q$. Substituting our expression for q gives:

$$p + q = p + (-2p) = -p$$

We are told that p is an integer greater than 1 ($p > 1$). Looking at the answer choices, the only value that fits the requirement that $p + q = -p$ where $p > 1$ is –5.

Things to Remember:

- If the zeros of a quadratic are given, it can be expressed as $y = a(x - p)(x - q)$.
- Expanding a factored expression allows you to directly compare terms to the standard form to identify unknown constants.

35. Correct Answer: $\frac{12}{5}$

The objective is to find the value of the constant k for the quadratic function given in vertex form: $h(x) = p(x - k)^2 - 10$, where $(k, -10)$ represents the vertex of the parabola.

Substitute the coordinates of the two points (0, 35) and (4, 10) into the function $h(x)$ and simplify to create a system of equations:

$$35 = p(0 - k)^2 - 10 \rightarrow 45 = k^2\, p$$

$$10 = p(4 - k)^2 - 10 \rightarrow 20 = p(4 - k)^2$$

Since we need to solve for k, we can eliminate p by dividing the first simplified equation by the second:

$$\frac{45 = k^2\,\text{p} - 10\text{p}}{20 = \text{p}(4 - k)^2} \rightarrow \frac{45}{20} = \frac{k^2\,\text{p}}{\text{p}(4 - k)^2} \rightarrow \frac{9}{4} = \frac{k^2}{(4 - k)^2}$$

To simplify the equation further, take the square root of both sides:

$$\sqrt{\left(\frac{9}{4}\right)} = \sqrt{\frac{k^2}{(4 - k)^2}}$$

$$\frac{3}{2} = \frac{k}{4 - k}$$

Cross multiply and solve for k:

$$\frac{3}{2} = \frac{k}{4 - k}$$

$3(4 - k) = 2k$	Cross-multiply
$12 - 3k = 2k$	Distribute
$12 = 5k$	Add
$k = \frac{12}{5}$	Divide

The final value for k is $\frac{12}{5}$.

Things to Remember:

- If given an equation and a point, plug-in to the equation to evaluate.

CONTINUE

36. Correct Answer: A. III only

For **exponential functions** of the form $y = ab^x$, if the function is increasing ($b > 1$), the **minimum** value for the domain $x \geq 0$ occurs at the **y-intercept** (where $x = 0$). Evaluate each option to determine the **minimum** value and if it is displayed in the given function.

The first function is defined as $m(x) = 25(1.2)^{x+4}$. Since the base (1.2) is greater than 1, the function is increasing. To find the minimum value, substitute $x = 0$ into the equation:

$$m(0) = 25(1.2)^{0+4}$$

$$m(0) = 25(1.2)^4$$

$$m(0) \approx 51.84$$

The value 51.84 is not displayed as a constant or coefficient in the original equation.

The next function is defined as $n(x) = 10(1.5)(0.8)^{x+2}$. Since the base (0.8) is between 0 and 1, this is a decreasing function. For a decreasing function, the y–intercept is the maximum value, not the minimum so this function is incorrect.

Note: Having ruled out I and II, it is safe to choose III only without solving completely though.

The last function is defined as $k(x) = 12(1.15)^x$. Since the base (1.15) is greater than 1, this is an increasing function. To find the minimum value, substitute $x = 0$ into the equation:

$$k(0) = 12(1.15)^0$$

$$k(0) = 12(1) = 12$$

The value 12 is explicitly shown as a coefficient in the equation. Therefore, only function III displays its minimum value for the given domain as a constant or coefficient.

Things to Remember:

- For exponential growth (base > 1) starting at $x = 0$, the y–intercept is the minimum. For exponential decay (base < 1) starting at $x = 0$, the y–intercept is the maximum.

37. Correct Answer: C. $f(x) = 600(0.85)^{\frac{x}{4}}$

The objective is to model a real–world scenario where a quantity decreases by a fixed percentage over a specific time interval using an **exponential function.**

The warehouse starts with 600 kilograms of the chemical. In the standard exponential form, $y = ab^{\frac{x}{t}}$, the variable "a" represents this starting amount:

$$y = 600b^{\frac{x}{t}}$$

The problem states the amount of chemical remaining decreases by 15 percent every 4 hours. To find the decay factor (b), subtract the percentage decrease (as a decimal) from 1:

$$1 - 0.15 = 0.85 = b$$

$$y = 600(0.85)^{\frac{x}{t}}$$

The decrease occurs every 4 hours, rather than every single hour. To ensure the decay factor is applied correctly when x represents total hours, the exponent must be divided by the length of the interval:

$$\frac{x}{t} = \frac{x}{4}$$

This gives the final function:

$$y = 600(0.85)^{\frac{x}{4}}$$

Things to Remember:

- For a percentage increase, the factor (b) is $1 + r$. For a percentage decrease, the factor is $1 - r$.
- The coefficient in front of the parentheses always represents the "initial" amount when time (or the exponent) is zero.

CONTINUE

38. Correct Answer: B. $5x^2 + 40x + 30b$

To determine which **quadratic** expression has $(x + 3b)$ as a **factor**, apply the **Factor Theorem**. According to the **Factor Theorem**, if $(x + 3b)$ is a factor of a **polynomial**, then substituting $x = -3b$ into that polynomial must result in zero.

For choice B, substituting $x = -3b$ into $5x^2 + 40x + 30b$ gives:

$5(-3b)^2 + 40(-3b) + 30b$	
$5(9b^2) - 120b + 30b$	Multiply
$45b^2 - 90b$	Simplify
$45b(b - 2)$	Factor

This equals 0 when $b = 2$, which is a positive integer. Verify this works, by replacing b with 2 in the original function:

$5x^2 + 40x + 30b$	
$5x^2 + 40x + 30(2)$	Substitute
$5x^2 + 40x + 60$	Multiply
$5(x^2 + 8x + 12)$	Factor
$5(x + 2)(x + 6)$	Factor

Since $3b = 3(2) = 6$, the factor $(x + 6)$ confirms that $(x + 3b)$ is indeed a factor.

Things to Remember:

- For any polynomial $P(x)$, if $(x - c)$ is a factor, then $P(c) = 0$.

37. Correct Answer: C. $f(x) = 600(0.85)^{\frac{x}{4}}$

The objective is to model a real–world scenario where a quantity decreases by a fixed percentage over a specific time interval using an **exponential function.**

The warehouse starts with 600 kilograms of the chemical. In the standard exponential form, $y = ab^{\frac{x}{t}}$, the variable "a" represents this starting amount:

$$y = 600b^{\frac{x}{t}}$$

The problem states the amount of chemical remaining decreases by 15 percent every 4 hours. To find the decay factor (b), subtract the percentage decrease (as a decimal) from 1:

$$1 - 0.15 = 0.85 = b$$

$$y = 600(0.85)^{\frac{x}{t}}$$

The decrease occurs every 4 hours, rather than every single hour. To ensure the decay factor is applied correctly when x represents total hours, the exponent must be divided by the length of the interval:

$$\frac{x}{t} = \frac{x}{4}$$

This gives the final function:

$$y = 600(0.85)^{\frac{x}{4}}$$

Things to Remember:

- For a percentage increase, the factor (b) is $1 + r$. For a percentage decrease, the factor is $1 - r$.
- The coefficient in front of the parentheses always represents the "initial" amount when time (or the exponent) is zero.

38. Correct Answer: B. $5x^2 + 40x + 30b$

To determine which **quadratic** expression has $(x + 3b)$ as a **factor**, apply the **Factor Theorem**. According to the **Factor Theorem**, if $(x + 3b)$ is a factor of a **polynomial**, then substituting $x = -3b$ into that polynomial must result in zero.

For choice B, substituting $x = -3b$ into $5x^2 + 40x + 30b$ gives:

$5(-3b)^2 + 40(-3b) + 30b$

$5(9b^2) - 120b + 30b$	Multiply
$45b^2 - 90b$	Simplify
$45b(b - 2)$	Factor

This equals 0 when $b = 2$, which is a positive integer. Verify this works, by replacing b with 2 in the original function:

$5x^2 + 40x + 30b$

$5x^2 + 40x + 30(2)$	Substitute
$5x^2 + 40x + 60$	Multiply
$5(x^2 + 8x + 12)$	Factor
$5(x + 2)(x + 6)$	Factor

Since $3b = 3(2) = 6$, the factor $(x + 6)$ confirms that $(x + 3b)$ is indeed a factor.

Things to Remember:

- For any polynomial $P(x)$, if $(x - c)$ is a factor, then $P(c) = 0$.

39. Correct Answer: B. $\frac{9}{4}$

To solve for x, isolate the variable and test values to determine what works. Begin with the provided equation and isolate x:

$$(x + \frac{1}{2})^2 - \frac{9}{4} = 0$$

$$(x + \frac{1}{2})^2 = \frac{9}{4}$$

$$x + \frac{1}{2} = \pm \frac{3}{2}$$

$$x = \pm \frac{3}{2} - \frac{1}{2}$$

$$x = 1 \text{ or } x = -2$$

The question asks for a "possible value" of $(x - \frac{5}{2})^2$ so test both values of x:

Using $x = 1$:

$$(1 - \frac{5}{2})^2 = (\frac{-3}{2})^2 = \frac{9}{4}$$

Using $x = -2$:

$$(-2 - \frac{5}{2})^2 = (\frac{-9}{2})^2 = \frac{81}{4}$$

Comparing these results to the answer choices, $\frac{9}{4}$ is listed as choice B.

Things to Remember:

- When you take the square root of both sides of an equation, always account for both the positive and negative roots.

CONTINUE

40. Correct Answer: D. 415

In mathematical modeling of **exponential functions** involving time, the "initial" state occurs at the exact moment the observation begins, which corresponds to $t = 0$.

The phrase "when it was set on the counter" refers to the starting time, so the value of the function T(t) needs to be evaluated at $t = 0$:

$T(t) = 300 + (415 - 300)(2.718)^{-0.12t}$

$T(0) = 300 + (415 - 300)(2.718)^{-0.12(0)}$ Substitute

$T(0) = 300 + (415 - 300)(2.718)^{0}$ Simplify

$T(0) = 300 + (415 - 300)$ Evaluate exponent

$T(0) = 415$ Simplify

The approximate temperature of the soup when it was set on the counter was 415 kelvins.

Things to Remember:

- In any function where time is the independent variable, the "initial" or "starting" value is found by evaluating the function at $t = 0$.

41. Correct Answer: B. 348

Since the solution of the given **quadratic** equation is given as a square root, this is a hint to use the **quadratic formula** to solve. First, identify each part of the equation that will be needed to fill in the quadratic formula. Factor out a 2 to make the numbers more manageable:

$$2(x^2 - 8x - 328) = 0$$

$$a = 1, b = -8, c = -328$$

Substitute these values into the quadratic formula $x = \frac{-b \pm \sqrt{b^2 - 4ac}}{2a}$:

$x = \frac{-(-8) \pm \sqrt{(-8)^2 - 4(1)(-328)}}{2(1)}$ Plug-in

$x = \frac{8 \pm \sqrt{64 + 1312}}{2}$ Simplify

$x = \frac{8 \pm \sqrt{1376}}{2}$ Add

$x = 4 \pm \frac{4\sqrt{344}}{2}$ Simplify

$x = 4 \pm \sqrt{344}$ Divide

By comparing the result to the form $x = h \pm \sqrt{k}$, $h = 4$ and $k = 344$. The question asks for the value of $h + k$:

$$4 + 344 = 348$$

Things to Remember:

- The quadratic formula $x = \frac{-b \pm \sqrt{b^2 - 4ac}}{2a}$ can be used to solve any quadratic equation that is not factorable.

42. Correct Answer: 20

The objective is to find the value of the expression $a - b$ for the **exponential function** $g(x) = a^x + b$. Use the given coordinates to solve for the unknown constants a and b.

The problem states that the graph has a **y-intercept** at (0, –11). This means when $x = 0$, $g(x) = -11$. Substitute these values into the function:

$$g(x) = a^x + b$$

$-11 = a^0 + b$	Substitute
$-11 = 1 + b$	Simplify
$-12 = b$	Subtract

Now, use the point (2, 52) to solve for a:

$$g(x) = a^x - 12$$

$$52 = a^2 - 12$$

$$64 = a^2$$

$$a = \pm 8$$

Since the problem specifies $a > 0$: $a = 8$. The question asks for the value of $a - b$:

$$8 - (-12) = 20$$

Things to Remember:

- Plug–in given values into an equation to solve for unknowns.

43. Correct Answer: 6

To find the value of t for which the estimated number of items in the warehouse, P(t), is exactly 362, substitute the given value for P(t) into the provided exponential function:

$$P(t) = 350(\frac{49}{50})^{t-6} + 12$$

$$362 = 350(\frac{49}{50})^{t-6} + 12$$

$$350 = 350(\frac{49}{50})^{t-6}$$

$$1 = (\frac{49}{50})^{t-6}$$

Since any number set to the power of 0 equals 1, set $t - 6 = 0$ to solve for t:

$$t - 6 = 0 \rightarrow t = 6$$

Therefore, the estimated number of items in the warehouse was 362 after 6 months.

Things to Remember:

- Always follow the order of operations in reverse (PEMDAS) when isolating a variable.

Radical Functions

44. Correct Answer: D. $b > a$

The problem states that the graph passes through the point (18, 0). This means that when $x = 18$, the function value $f(x)$ is 0:

$$0 = a\sqrt{b - 18}$$

For the product of two terms to be zero, at least one of the terms must be zero. Since $f(-2) < 0$, a cannot be 0, which means the square root term must be zero:

$\sqrt{b - 18} = 0$

$b - 18 = 0$	Square both sides
$b = 18$	Add

Since $b = 18$, use the inequality $f(-2) < 0$ to find the sign of a:

$$f(-2) = a\sqrt{18 - (-2)}$$

$$f(-2) = a\sqrt{20}$$

We are given that $f(-2)$ is negative ($f(-2) < 0$). Since the principal square root of 20 is a positive number, the constant a must be negative for the overall product to be negative.

Since 18 is a positive integer and a is a negative number, b must be greater than a. This matches Choice D.

Things to Remember:

- If the product of two factors is zero, at least one factor must be zero. This is essential for finding intercepts in radical and polynomial functions.

Radical Functions

45. Correct Answer: 8

The objective is to find the greatest integer value for k such that the radical equation $\sqrt{5x + k} = x + 3$ has no real solutions. This involves transforming the radical equation into a quadratic equation and analyzing its discriminant.

Square both sides of the equation to remove the square root:

$(\sqrt{5x + k})^2 = (x + 3)^2$	Square both sides
$5x + k = (x + 3)^2$	Simplify
$5x + k = x^2 + 6x + 9$	FOIL

Move all terms to one side of the equation to set it equal to zero:

$5x + k = x^2 + 6x + 9$

$0 = x^2 + x + 9 - k$

For a **quadratic equation** $ax^2 + bx + c = 0$ to have **no real solutions**, its **discriminant** must be less than zero.

Identify the coefficients from the equation: $a = 1$, $b = 1$, $c = 9 - k$. Set the discriminant to be less than zero, then solve for k:

$b^2 - 4ac < 0$

$1^2 - 4(1)(9 - k) < 0$	Substitute
$1 - 36 + 4k < 0$	Distribute
$-35 + 4k < 0$	Simplify
$4k < 35$	Add
$k < (35)/4$	Divide
$k < 8.75$	Simplify

The question states that k is an integer constant and asks for the greatest possible value of k such that $k < 8.75$. The largest integer that satisfies this condition is 8.

Things to Remember:

- For $ax^2 + bx + c = 0$, the discriminant is $b^2 - 4ac$. If it is greater than 0, there are two real solutions; if it equals 0, there is one real solution; and if it is less than 0, there are no real solutions.
- Always pay attention to the term "integer." If your result is a decimal like 8.75 and you need the greatest integer "less than" that value, you must round down to the nearest whole number.

CONTINUE

46. Correct Answer: D. 36

The model is given by the function $E(t) = 500(1.02)^{\frac{t}{3}}$. In an exponential growth model $y = a(1 + r)^{\frac{t}{k}}$:

- a is the initial value (500 watt-hours).
- r is the growth rate (0.02, which represents a 2% increase).
- t is the total time passed in years.
- k is the time interval required for the growth rate r to occur exactly once.

By looking at the exponent $\frac{t}{3}$, we can see that the growth factor of 1.02 (the 2% increase) is applied once every time t increases by 3. When $t = 3$ years, the exponent is $\frac{3}{3} = 1$, meaning the energy has increased by 2% exactly once. Therefore, the energy increases by 2% every 3 years.

The question specifically asks for the value of m months. To convert the time interval from years to months:

$$3 \text{ years} \times 12 \text{ months per year} = 36 \text{ months}$$

Thus, $m = 36$.

Things to Remember:

- In the form $y = a(b)^{\frac{t}{k}}$, the base b represents the total change factor that happens over the time period k.
- Always check the units provided for the variables (years) versus the units requested in the final answer (months).

47. Correct Answer: B. The capacity is approximately 25 watt–hours 4 half-life periods (80 years) after it begins operation.

The goal is to interpret the meaning of $C(4 \cdot 20) = 25$ in the context of the function $C(t) = 400(0.5)^{\frac{t}{20}}$.

First, evaluate the input. The expression $C(4 \cdot 20)$ means $C(80)$, so we are finding the capacity at $t = 80$ years after the satellite begins operation.

Next, understand the structure of the function. The base 0.5 indicates exponential decay with a half-life. The exponent $\frac{t}{20}$ tells us that the half–life is 20 years, meaning the capacity is halved every 20 years. Therefore, 80 years represents $\frac{80}{20} = 4$ half–life periods.

Therefore, the equation $C(4 \cdot 20) = 25$ tells us that after 4 half–life periods (which equals 80 years), the battery capacity has decreased to approximately 25 watt–hours.

Things to Remember:

- In any modeling question, always identify what the independent variable (input) and dependent variable (output) represent in real–world.

48. Correct Answer: C. 77

To solve, use the give points and the **standard exponential model** to evaluate the values of a and b.

The graph passes through the point (0, 11). This point represents the **y–intercept** of the function. Substitute $t = 0$ and $A(0) = 11$ into the equation:

$A(t) = a \cdot b^t$	
$11 = a \cdot b^0$	Substitute
$11 = a$	Simplify

Given $a = 11$, the function can now be written as $A(t) = 11b^t$. Use the second given point, (2, 539), where $t = 2$ and $A(2) = 539$, to find the value of b:

$A(t) = 11b^t$	
$539 = 11b^2$	Substitute
$49 = b^2$	Divide
$7 = b$	Square root, $b > 0$

The question asks for the product of a and b:

$$ab = 11 \times 7$$
$$ab = 77$$

This corresponds to choice C.

Things to Remember:

- In an exponential function of the form $y = a \cdot b^x$, the constant "a" represents the y–intercept (the value when $x = 0$).
- Any non–zero base raised to the power of zero equals 1.

Graph Transformation of Polynomial Functions

49. Correct Answer: C. $g(x)=f(\frac{x}{3})$

The goal is to determine which transformation of the function $f(x)$ results in a new function, $g(x)$, that increases by 50 percent for every 3-unit increase in x.

The original function is defined as $f(x) = k(1.5)^x$. The base 1.5 represents a 50 percent increase (1.0 + 0.5 = 1.5). Because the exponent is simply x, this 50 percent increase occurs every time x increases by 1.

The problem requires $g(x)$ to also increase by 50 percent, meaning the base of the exponential term must remain 1.5. However, this increase should now happen every time x increases by 3.

In exponential modeling, if a rate occurs over a period of p units, the exponent is written as $\frac{x}{p}$. To make the 50 percent increase happen every 3 units, the function $g(x)$ should be:

$$g(x) = k(1.5)^{\frac{x}{3}}$$

Compare the target function for $g(x)$ to the original definition of $f(x)$:

$$f(x) = k(1.5)^x$$
$$g(x) = k(1.5)^{\frac{x}{3}}$$

By looking at the exponents, it is clear that $g(x)$ is the function f evaluated at $\frac{x}{3}$ instead of x. Therefore, the correct transformation is $g(x) = f(\frac{x}{3})$.

Things to Remember:

- In the form $y = a(b)^{\frac{x}{p}}$, the base b is the growth or decay factor, and p is the interval of x required for that factor to be applied once.
- Replacing x with $\frac{x}{c}$ in a function results in a horizontal stretch by a factor of c.

SOLUTIONS
NONLINEAR FUNCTIONS

Zeros, Factors, and Factored Form Polynomial Functions

50. Correct Answer: B. $4x^3 + 18x^2 + 18kx$

The goal is to find which expression has $(x + 3k)$ as a factor, where k is a positive integer constant.

If $(x + 3k)$ is a factor of an expression, then substituting $x = -3k$ must make the expression equal to 0. Test each answer choice by substituting $x = -3k$ and checking if the result equals 0 for some positive integer value of k.

For choice B, substituting $x = -3k$ into $4x^3 + 18x^2 + 18kx$ gives:

$4(-3k)^3 + 18(-3k)^2 + 18k(-3k)$	Substitute
$4(-27k^3) + 18(9k^2) - 54k^2$	Multiply
$-108k^3 + 162k^2 - 54k^2$	Simplify
$-108k^3 + 108k^2$	Combine terms
$108k^2(1 - k)$	Factor

This equals 0 when $k = 1$, which is a positive integer.

Things to Remember:

- If $(x + a)$ is a factor of a polynomial, then substituting $x = -a$ makes the polynomial equal to 0.

51. Correct Answer: A. $N = 250(3)^{\frac{t}{45}}$

The problem states the backup system starts with 250 copies. In the standard **exponential growth** formula $y = ab^x$, the constant "a" represents this starting amount. Therefore, $a = 250$:

$$N = 250b^x$$

Tripling every 45 minutes means a growth factor of 3 once per 45 minutes. This multiplier is the base "b" of the exponential term. Therefore, $b = 3$:

$$N = 250(3)^x$$

The tripling effect happens once every 45 minutes. If t is in minutes, the exponent should be $\frac{t}{45}$. This ensures that when $t = 45$, the exponent equals 1, and the initial value is multiplied by the growth factor exactly once. The resulting equation is:

$$N = 250(3)^{\frac{t}{45}}$$

This matches Choice A.

Things to Remember:

- Exponential growth is often modeled as $y = ab^x$.
- The exponent needs to reflect the actual time it takes for the multiplier to occur.

CONTINUE

52. Correct Answer: D. 168

The goal is to determine the value of the expression $f(3) - f(1)$ by identifying the quadratic function $g(x)$ and then applying its relationship to the **composite function** $f(x)$.

Create the equation for $g(x)$ using **vertex form**. The problem states that $g(x)$ is a **quadratic function** with a **vertex** at $(-2, 7)$. The vertex form of a quadratic function is $g(x) = a(x - h)^2 + k$, where (h, k) is the vertex. Substitute the vertex $(-2, 7)$ into the formula:

$$g(x) = a(x + 2)^2 + 7$$

Evaluate the constant a using the given point $(0, 31)$.

$31 = a(0 + 2)^2 + 7$	Substitute
$31 = 4a + 7$	Simplify
$24 = 4a$	Subtract
$a = 6$	Divide

The complete function is $g(x) = 6(x + 2)^2 + 7$.

The problem defines $f(x)$ as the composite function $g(x + 3)$. To find $f(3)$, substitute $x = 3$ into the relationship:

$$f(3) = g(3 + 3) = g(6)$$

$$g(6) = 6(6 + 2)^2 + 7 = 6(8)^2 + 7 = 384 + 7 = 391$$

To find $f(1)$, substitute $x = 1$ into the relationship:

$$f(1) = g(1 + 3) = g(4)$$

$$g(4) = 6(4 + 2)^2 + 7 = 6(6)^2 + 7 = 216 + 7 = 223$$

Calculate the final value of $g(6) - g(4)$:

$$391 - 223 = 168$$

Things to Remember:

- Use $y = a(x - h)^2 + k$ whenever you are given the vertex of a parabola.

53. Correct Answer: 60

To find the minimum possible value of $3m$, convert the **radical** equation into a **quadratic** form and analyze its **discriminant.**

To solve the equation, square both sides to remove the radical and then move all terms to one side to set the equation equal to zero:

$\sqrt{m - 2x} = x - 10$

$m - 2x = (x - 10)^2$	Square both sides
$m - 2x = x^2 - 20x + 100$	FOIL
$0 = x^2 - 18x + 100 - m$	Set equal to 0

For a **quadratic equation** to have exactly **one real solution,** the **discriminant** (b^2 - 4ac) must equal zero. Plug-in the values from the new expression to evaluate m:

$$(-18)^2 - 4(1)(100 - m) = 0$$

$$324 - 400 + 4m = 0$$

$$-76 + 4m = 0$$

$$4m = 76$$

$$m = 19$$

If $m = 19$, the equation is $x - 18x + 100 - m$. This factors to $(x - 9)2 = 0$, so $x = 9$. Since 9 is less than 10, this solution is extraneous.

Because $m = 19$ results in an invalid (extraneous) solution, m must be slightly larger to produce a valid solution where x is at least 10. The smallest integer value for m that satisfies the requirement is 20.

Use $m = 20$ to evaluate the minimum possible value of $3m$:

$$3m = 3(20) = 60$$

Things to Remember:

- For a quadratic equation, the discriminant is $b^2 - 4ac$. It determines the number of real solutions ($D > 0$ has two, $D = 0$ has one, $D < 0$ has none).
- When a problem asks for a "minimum" and the boundary value doesn't work, look for the next valid integer.

Standard Form Polynomial Functions

54. Correct Answer: B. –54

The problem provides the **x–intercepts** of a **parabola** and asks for a **y–intercept** based on specific constraints for the constant a.

Start by using the **x–intercepts** to write the equation in **factored form.** If the intercepts are at $x = -3$ and $x = 9$, the factors of the quadratic are $(x + 3)$ and $(x - 9)$. This gives the equation:

$$f(x) = a(x + 3)(x - 9)$$

To find the y-intercept, evaluate the function at $x = 0$:

$f(0) = a(0 + 3)(0 - 9)$	Plug-in
$f(0) = a(3)(-9)$	Simplify
$f(0) = -27a$	Multiply

The problem states that a is an integer and $0 < a \leq 2$. This means a can only be 1 or 2. Calculate the possible y-intercepts for both values:

- If $a = 1 \rightarrow$ y–intercept $= -27(1) = -27$
- If $a = 2 \rightarrow$ y–intercept $= -27(2) = -54$

Comparing these results to the given choices, only –54 is listed as a possible option.

Things to Remember:

- The factored form of a quadratic is $y = a(x - r_1)(x - r_2)$, where r_1 and r_2 are the x–intercepts.
- To find the y-intercept of any function, substitute $x = 0$ into the equation and solve for y.
- In the standard form $y = ax^2 + bx + c$, the constant c always represents the y–intercept (the value of the function when $x = 0$).

55. Correct Answer: B. 5

The problem asks for the sum of all real solutions to a rational equation. To solve this, you must identify which values of x make the numerator equal to zero while ensuring those values do not make the denominator zero.

First, examine the given equation:

$$\frac{(x-6)(x+1)(x-3)}{(x-3)(x-8)} = 0$$

Notice that the term $(x - 3)$ appears in both the numerator and the denominator. The expression can be simplified by canceling these terms, but keep in mind that x cannot equal 3, as this would result in division by zero (an undefined value).

After canceling $(x - 3)$, the equation becomes:

$$\frac{(x-6)(x+1)}{(x-8)} = 0$$

A fraction is equal to zero only when its numerator is zero. Set each factor in the numerator to zero to find the potential solutions:

$$x - 6 = 0 \rightarrow x = 6$$

$$x + 1 = 0 \rightarrow x = -1$$

Check these solutions against the denominator. Since neither 6 nor –1 makes the denominator $(x - 8)$ equal to zero, both are valid real solutions.

Finally, calculate the sum of these real solutions:

$$6 + (-1) = 5$$

Things to Remember:

- A rational expression is equal to zero only when the numerator equals zero.
- Extraneous solutions occur when a value makes the numerator zero but also makes the denominator zero; these must be excluded.
- Always check that your solutions do not result in division by zero in the original equation.

CONTINUE

56. Correct Answer: B. $x + 4$

To find the factors, look for common terms that can be factored out to simplify the expression.

First, identify the greatest common factor (GCF) shared by both parts of the expression. Both terms contain the number 12 and at least one $(x + 20)$ group. Factoring these out gives:

$$12(x + 20)(x^2 - (x + 20))$$

Next, simplify the expression inside the brackets. It is important to distribute the negative sign to both terms inside the parentheses:

$$12(x + 20)(x^2 - x - 20)$$

Now, factor the quadratic expression $x^2 - x - 20$:

$$12(x + 20)(x - 5)(x + 4)$$

The complete list of linear factors for this expression is $(x + 20)$, $(x - 5)$, and $(x + 4)$. Comparing these to the given answer choices, only $x + 4$ matches.

Things to Remember:

- Always look for a Greatest Common Factor (GCF) first to simplify complex expressions.
- When factoring out a group, treat it as a single unit.

57. Correct Answer: 4

The problem provides a table of values for a rational function and asks for the value of the constant k. To find this, pick any point (x, y) from the table and substitute it into the given equation.

The most efficient point to use is (7, 0) because a y-value of 0 simplifies the calculation significantly. Substitute $x = 7$ and $f(x) = 0$ into the equation:

$$f(x) = \frac{kx - 28}{x - 5}$$

$$0 = \frac{(k(7) - 28)}{7 - 5}$$

$$0 = \frac{(7k - 28)}{2}$$

For a fraction to equal zero, its numerator must be zero. Set the numerator equal to zero to solve for k:

$7k - 28 = 0$

$7k = 28$ Add

$k = 4$ Divide

Things to Remember:

- A rational function equals zero when its numerator is zero, provided the denominator is non-zero at that point.
- To find a missing constant in a function, substitute known values for x and y from a table or graph and solve the resulting equation.

Exponential Functions

58. Correct Answer: A. 100(S – 1)

For the given **exponential equation**, the variable m represents minutes, but the growth rate is asked for in seconds. Start by converting 180 seconds into minutes:

$$\frac{180 \text{ seconds}}{60 \text{ seconds per minute}} = 3 \text{ minutes}$$

Next, determine the growth factor for a 3-minute interval. Looking at the exponent in the model and notice that when 3 minutes pass (meaning m increases by 3), the exponent increases by exactly 1:

$$P(m + 3) = 80 \cdot S^{\frac{m+3}{3}}$$

$$P(m + 3) = 80 \cdot S^{\frac{m}{3}+1}$$

$$P(m + 3) = 80 \cdot S^{\frac{m}{3}} \cdot S^{1}$$

This shows that every 3 minutes, the current population is multiplied by the constant S. In exponential growth models, the multiplier is equal to $(1 + r)$, where r is the decimal rate of increase. To find the percentage p, set up the following relationship:

$$1 + \frac{p}{100} = S$$

$$\frac{p}{100} = S - 1$$

$$p = 100(S - 1)$$

Things to Remember:

- Ensure time units (seconds vs. minutes) are consistent across the entire problem.
- In an exponential function $y = ab^{\frac{t}{k}}$, the value b represents the growth factor that occurs every k units of time.
- To convert a growth factor b to a percentage increase p, use $p = 100(b - 1)$.

59. Correct Answer: 409

The problem describes the motion of a projectile and asks for its height at a specific time. Since the initial launch height and the maximum height (the vertex) are given this suggests that **vertex form** is the most efficient way to model this **quadratic** function.

A quadratic function in vertex form is written as $h(t) = a(t - h)^2 + k$, where (h, k) is the vertex. The problem states the maximum height is 625 feet at 5 seconds, so the vertex is (5, 625). Substitute these values into the formula:

$$h(t) = a(t - h)^2 + k \rightarrow h(t) = a(t - 5)^2 + 625$$

Next, find the value of the constant a using the launch information. The projectile was launched from 25 feet at 0 seconds, giving you the point (0, 25). Substitute $t = 0$ and $h(t) = 25$ into your equation to solve for a:

$25 = a(0 - 5)^2 + 625$

$25 = a(5)^2 + 625$	Simplify
$25 = 25a + 625$	Square
$-600 = 25a$	Subtract
$a = -24$	Divide

This creates the final **quadratic** model:

$$h(t) = -24(t - 5)^2 + 625$$

To calculate the height at $t = 2$ seconds, plug–in 2:

$h(2) = -24(2 - 5)^2 + 625$

$h(2) = -24(-3)^2 + 625$	Simplify
$h(2) = -24(9) + 625$	Square
$h(2) = -216 + 625$	Multiply
$h(2) = 409$	Add

The height of the projectile 2 seconds after launch was 409 feet.

Things to Remember:

- Use the vertex form $y = a(x - h)^2 + k$ when you are given the maximum or minimum point of a quadratic.

CONTINUE

60. Correct Answer: 1000

To solve this question efficiently, it is important to recognize the symmetry in the function $p(x) = k((x-2)^2-m)((x-2)^2-n)$. Since the function replaces the x variable with $(x-2)^2$, any two x-values that produce the same value of $(x-2)^2$ will give the same output.

Since both $x = -2$ and $x = 6$ produce the same value of $(x-2)^2 = 16$, we know that $p(-2) = p(6)$.

The problem states that the graph passes through the point (6, 500), which means $p(6) = 500$. Therefore, $p(-2) = 500$ as well. Add these together to get the final answer:

$$p(-2) + p(6) = 500 + 500 = 1000$$

Things to Remember:

- When a quadratic function is given in x–intercept form, the function is symmetric about the x–intercepts.
- Two x–values equidistant from the axis of symmetry will produce the same output.

ADVANCED MATH

61 NONLINEAR EQUATIONS & SYSTEMS OF EQUATIONS

$$(x - m)^2 = (2m - 3t)(x - m)$$

In the given equation, m and t are constants where $m > \frac{3t}{2}$. The sum of the solutions to the equation is $4m + 27$. What is the value of t?

62 NONLINEAR EQUATIONS & SYSTEMS OF EQUATIONS

In the xy–plane, the graph of $y = f(x)$ has exactly 9 x–intercepts. One of these x-intercepts is at (4, 0) and another is at (–2, 0). The rational function g is defined by the equation $g(x) = \frac{f(x)}{(x-4)(x+2)}$. In the xy–plane, how many x-intercepts does the graph of $y = g(x)$ have?

63 NONLINEAR EQUATIONS & SYSTEMS OF EQUATIONS

The exponential function f is defined by $f(x) = ab^x$, where a and b are positive constants. If $f(s) = t$ and $f(s + 3) = t - 0.488t$, where s and t are constants, what is the value of b?

A. 0.20

B. 0.51

C. 0.80

D. 1.51

64 NONLINEAR EQUATIONS & SYSTEMS OF EQUATIONS

Function f is a quadratic function. The graph of $y = f(x)$ in the xy–plane has a vertex at (2, –3), contains the point (4, 5), and has a y–intercept at (0, b). The graph of $y = 7 \cdot f(x)$ has a y–intercept at (0, c). What is the positive difference between b and c?

65 NONLINEAR EQUATIONS & SYSTEMS OF EQUATIONS

$$\frac{1}{kx} = \frac{x}{64} + \frac{1}{k}$$

In the given equation, k is a nonzero constant. If the equation has exactly one real solution for x, what is the value of k?

66 NONLINEAR EQUATIONS & SYSTEMS OF EQUATIONS

$$y = 3x^2 - 18x + 29$$

$$y = 2x + k$$

In the given system of equations, k is a constant. The graphs of the equations in the given system intersect at exactly one point (x, y) in the xy-plane. What is the value of x at the point of intersection?

67 NONLINEAR EQUATIONS & SYSTEMS OF EQUATIONS

$$y = 2x - k$$

$$y = -8(x - 10)^2$$

In the given system of equations, k is a constant. The system has two distinct real solutions. Which of the following could be the value of k?

A. 5

B. 9

C. $\frac{15}{98}$

D. 21

68 NONLINEAR EQUATIONS & SYSTEMS OF EQUATIONS

$$f(x) = x - 3$$

$$g(x) = 4x^2 + px + q$$

The functions f and g are given in function g, p and q are constants. If $f(x) \cdot g(x) = 4$ x 3 – 108 for all real x, what is the value of p?

ADVANCED MATH

69 NONLINEAR EQUATIONS & SYSTEMS OF EQUATIONS

$$\frac{32x}{x^2 - 16} = \frac{x}{x - 4} + \frac{24}{x + 4}$$

What is the positive solution to the given equation?

70 NONLINEAR EQUATIONS & SYSTEMS OF EQUATIONS

$$(x) = \sqrt[3]{(x - 5)^2} + 18$$

$$h(x) = \sqrt{324 + x^2 - 36x}$$

The functions g and h are defined by the given equations. If $g(8) = t$, where t is a constant, what is the value of $h(t)$?

A. 9

B. $\sqrt[3]{9}$

C. $\sqrt[3]{9} + 18$

D. 27

71 NONLINEAR EQUATIONS & SYSTEMS OF EQUATIONS

$$x(ax - 30) = -12$$

In the given equation, a is an integer constant. If the equation has two distinct real solutions, what is the greatest possible value of a?

72 NONLINEAR EQUATIONS & SYSTEMS OF EQUATIONS

The function p is defined by $p(x) = 48x - 3x^2$. The function q is defined by $q(x) = p(x) + 2$. Which expression represents the maximum value of $q(x)$?

A. $386 - 3(\frac{48}{6})^2$

B. $386 + (\frac{48}{6})^2$

C. $128 - (\frac{48}{6})^2$

D. $384 - 3(\frac{48}{2})^2$

CONTINUE

ADVANCED MATH

73 NONLINEAR EQUATIONS & SYSTEMS OF EQUATIONS

$$y = -3x^2 + 12x + 5$$

$$y = 2x + b$$

In the system where b is a constant, the graphs intersect at exactly one point (x, y) in the xy-plane. What is the value of x at that point?

A. 1

B. $\frac{10}{3}$

C. $\frac{5}{3}$

D. 4

74 NONLINEAR EQUATIONS & SYSTEMS OF EQUATIONS

$$\frac{1}{x+2} + \frac{1}{x-4} = \frac{12}{x^2 - 2x - 8}$$

What are all the solutions to the given equation?

A. –2 and 4

B. 1 and 7

C. –2

D. 7

75 NONLINEAR EQUATIONS & SYSTEMS OF EQUATIONS

$$x(8x - 3a) + b(8x - 3a) - (x + b) = 0$$

In the given equation, a and b are positive constants. A solution to the equation is $x = 15$. What is the value of a?

SEE SOLUTIONS ON NEXT PAGE

CONTINUE

ANSWER KEY

QUESTIONS 61-75	
61	-9
62	7
63	C
64	30
65	-16
66	10/3
67	D
68	12
69	12
70	B
71	18
72	A
73	B
74	D
75	119/3

61. Correct Answer: –9

To find the value of t, move all terms to one side to set the equation to zero:

$$(x - m)^2 = (2m - 3t)(x - m)$$

$$(x - m)^2 - (2m - 3t)(x - m) = 0$$

Now, factor out the common term $(x - m)$:

$$(x - m - (2m - 3t))(x - m) = 0$$

Simplify the expression inside the brackets:

$$(x - 3m + 3t)(x - m) = 0$$

To find the **solutions** (roots), set each **factor** equal to zero:

$$x - 3m + 3t = 0 \rightarrow x = 3m - 3t$$

$$x - m = 0 \rightarrow x = m$$

The problem states that the sum of these solutions is $4m + 27$, so set up an equation for the sum:

$m + (3m - 3t) = 4m + 27$

$4m - 3t = 4m + 27$	Simplify
$-3t = 27$	Cancel $4m$
$t = -9$	Divide

Things to Remember:

- When solving equations by factoring, set the equation to zero first.

CONTINUE

62. Correct Answer: 7

The graph of $y = f(x)$ has 9 x–intercepts. In a **polynomial** function, an **x–intercept** at $(k, 0)$ corresponds to a **factor** of $(x - k)$ in the function. Since it is given that two of these intercepts are $(4, 0)$ and $(-2, 0)$, then $f(x)$ must contain the factors $(x - 4)$ and $(x + 2)$.

If the factors of $f(x)$ are plugged into $g(x) = \frac{f(x)}{(x-4)(x+2)}$, the $(x - 4)$ and $(x + 2)$ terms in the numerator will be cancelled out by the same terms in the denominator.

In a rational function, when a factor appears in both the numerator and the denominator, it creates a "hole" (removable discontinuity) in the graph rather than an x–intercept. Because these two specific intercepts are removed (cancelled), the number of x–intercepts for $g(x)$ will be the original number of intercepts minus the two that were cancelled:

$$9 - 2 = 7$$

Things to Remember:

- An x–intercept of a function $f(x)$ occurs where the numerator is zero, provided that the denominator is not also zero at that same point.
- Factors that are common to both the numerator and denominator of a rational function represent holes in the graph, not x–intercepts or vertical asymptotes.

63. Correct Answer: C. 0.80

The **exponential function** $f(x) = ab^x$ and two specific conditions are given. To solve for b, first substitute the given conditions into the general form of the function:

$$f(s) = t \rightarrow t = ab^s$$

$$f(s+3) = t - 0.488t = 0.512t \rightarrow 0.512t = ab^{(s+3)}$$

Using the properties of exponents, rewrite the second equation as a multiplication statement:

$$0.512t = ab^{(s+3)}$$

$$0.512t = ab^s \times b^3$$

Now, substitute the first equation into this rewritten equation:

$0.512t = ab^s \times b^3$

$0.512t = t \times b^3$

Now, solve for b:

$0.512t = tb^3$

$0.512 = b^3$ Cancel t

b =0.80 Cube root

Things to Remember:

- Use exponent rules to break apart sums in exponents: $b(x + y) = (bx)(by)$.

Vertex Form Equation of a Parabola

64. Correct Answer: 30

Begin by finding the equation for the **quadratic function** $f(x)$. Since the vertex is given as (2, –3), use the **vertex form:**

$$f(x) = a(x - h)^2 + k$$

$$f(x) = a(x - 2)^2 - 3$$

To find the value of a, plug in the point (4, 5):

$5 = a(4 - 2)^2 - 3$	Plug-in
$5 = a(2)^2 - 3$	Subtract
$5 = 4a - 3$	Simplify
$8 = 4a$	Add
$a = 2$	Divide

The **y-intercept** of $f(x)$ is b. To find it, set $x = 0$:

$b = f(0) = 2(0 - 2)^2 - 3$	Plug-in
$b = 2(4) - 3$	Subtract
$b = 5$	Simplify

Next, look at the second function: $y = 7f(x)$. The **y-intercept** of this function is c. To find this, set $x = 0$:

$c = 7 \times f(0)$	
$c = 7 \times 5$	Substitute
$c = 35$	Multiply

The question asks for the positive difference between b and c:

$$|35 - 5| = 30$$

Things to Remember:

- Vertex form of a quadratic is $f(x) = a(x - h)^2 + k$, where (h, k) is the vertex.
- To find any y–intercept, always set x equal to 0.

Rational Equations

65. Correct Answer: –16

To solve for x, first eliminate the denominators by multiplying the entire equation by the **least common multiple**, which is $64kx$:

$$\left(\frac{1}{kx} = \frac{x}{64} + \frac{1}{k}\right) \times 64kx \rightarrow 64 = kx^2 + 64x$$

Next, rearrange the equation into the **standard quadratic** form by subtracting 64 from both sides:

$$0 = kx^2 + 64x - 64$$

The problem states that there is exactly one real solution for x. For a quadratic equation to have exactly one real solution, its **discriminant** must be equal to zero. Use the coefficients $a = k$, $b = 64$, $c = -64$:

$64^2 - 4(k)(-64) = 0$	Plug-in
$4096 + 256k = 0$	Multiply
$256k = -4096$	Subtract
$k = -16$	Divide

Things to Remember:

- To clear fractions in an equation, multiply every term by the common denominator.
- The discriminant determines the number of real solutions.

66. Correct Answer: $\frac{10}{3}$

To find the intersection point of the system, set the two equations equal to each other:

$$3x^2 - 18x + 29 = 2x + k$$

Move all terms to one side to set the equation to zero:

$$3x^2 - 20x + 29 - k = 0$$

The problem specifies that the graphs intersect at "exactly one point". This means the resulting quadratic equation has only one solution for x. In a quadratic that has only one solution, that solution must be the x-coordinate of the vertex. The x-coordinate of the vertex for any quadratic is found using the formula $\frac{-b}{2a}$:

$$x = \frac{-b}{2a} = \frac{-(-20)}{2(3)} = \frac{20}{6} = \frac{10}{3}$$

Note: While you could solve for k using the discriminant and then solve for x, using the vertex formula directly is a much faster shortcut when you only need the x-value.

Things to Remember:

- When a line is tangent to a parabola (intersecting at exactly one point), the intersection occurs at the solution of the combined quadratic.
- The x-coordinate of a single-solution quadratic is always $\frac{-b}{2a}$.

SOLUTIONS

NONLINEAR EQUATIONS & SYSTEMS OF EQUATIONS

67. Correct Answer: D. 21

To find the number of solutions for the system, set the equations equal to each other:

$$2x - k = -8(x - 10)^2$$

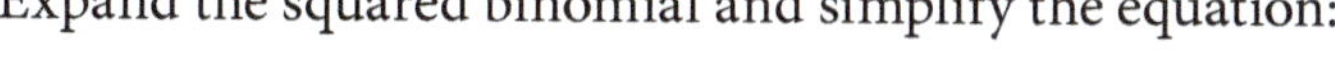

Expand the squared binomial and simplify the equation:

$$2x - k = -8(x^2 - 20x + 100)$$

$$2x - k = -8x^2 + 160x - 800$$

Move all terms to one side to form a quadratic equation equal to zero:

$$2x - k = -8x^2 + 160x - 800$$

$$0 = -8x^2 + 158x - 800 + k$$

The system has "two distinct real solutions," meaning the discriminant must be greater than zero ($b^2 - 4ac > 0$). Use a = –8, b = 158, and c = –800 + k to evaluate k:

$b^2 - 4ac > 0$	
$(158)^2 - 4(-8)(-800 + k) > 0$	Plug-in
$24964 - 25600 + 32k > 0$	Multiply
$-636 + 32k > 0$	Subtract
$-32k > 636$	Add
$k > 19.875$	Divide

Looking at the answer choices, only 21 is greater than 19.875.

Things to Remember:

- "Two distinct real solutions" for a system involving a quadratic always points toward using the discriminant > 0.

68. Correct Answer: 12

To evaluate p in the given equation, multiply $f(x)$ and $g(x)$ and set it equal to the given expression. Start by multiplying $f(x)$ and $g(x)$:

$f(x) \cdot g(x)$	
$(x - 3)(4x^2 + px + q)$	Substitute
$4x^3 - 12x^2 + px^2 - 3px + qx - 3q$	Expand

Set this expression equal to the one given and then match the coefficients to evaluate p. Since there are no x^2 terms in the other expression, set the x^2 from $f(x) \cdot g(x)$ equal to 0 and the solve for p:

$$4x^3 - 12x^2 + px^2 - 3px + qx - 3q = 4x^3 - 108$$

$$-12x^2 + px^2 = 0$$

$$px^2 = 12x^2$$

$$p = 12$$

Things to Remember:

- If two polynomials are equal for all values of x, their corresponding coefficients must be identical.

Rational Equations

69. Correct Answer: 12

To solve for x, first find a **common denominator** for all terms. Notice that the denominator on the left side, $x^2 - 16$, is a **difference of squares** that factors into $(x - 4)(x + 4)$. This matches the denominators on the right side. Rewrite the equation with a common denominator of $(x - 4)(x + 4)$:

$$\frac{32x}{x^2 - 16} = \frac{x}{x - 4} + \frac{24}{x + 4} \rightarrow \frac{32x}{(x - 4)(x + 4)} = \frac{x(x + 4)}{(x - 4)(x + 4)} + \frac{(24(x - 4)}{(x - 4)(x + 4)}$$

Since the denominators all match, focus on the numerators and then simplify to solve for x:

$32x = x(x + 4) + 24(x - 4)$	Isolate numerators
$32x = x^2 + 4x + 24x - 96$	Distribute
$32x = x^2 + 28x - 96$	Simplify
$0 = x^2 - 4x - 96$	Subtract

The **quadratic** must now be factored to evaluate the solution:

$0 = x^2 - 4x - 96$

$0 = (x - 12)(x + 8)$

Set each factor equal to 0 to solve:

$$x - 12 = 0 \rightarrow x = 12$$

$$x + 8 = 0 \rightarrow x = -8$$

The question asks for the positive solution, so the answer is 12.

Things to Remember:

- Always check if denominators can be factored (like the difference of squares) to find the least common denominator.

Expressions with Square Root

70. Correct Answer: B. $\sqrt[3]{9}$

The problem asks for the value of $h(t)$, where $t = g(8)$ so first find the value of t by evaluating $g(8)$:

$$g(x) = \sqrt[3]{(x-5)^2\,)} + 18$$

$g(8) = \sqrt{(8-5)^2} + 18$	Substitute
$g(8) = \sqrt[3]{(3)^2} + 18$	Subtract
$g(8) = \sqrt[3]{9} + 18$	Square

Before plugging-in $g(8)$, simplify $h(x)$:

$$h(x) = \sqrt{324 + x^2 - 36x}$$

$h(x) = \sqrt{x^2 - 36x + 324}$	Reorder terms
$h(x) = \sqrt{(x-18)^2}$	Factor
$h(x) = x - 18$	Square root

Now, plug-in g(8) into h(x) and simplify:

$h(g(8)) = \sqrt[3]{9} + 18 - 18$	Plug-in
$h(g(8)) = \sqrt[3]{9}$	Simplify

Things to Remember:

- In composite function problems, simplify the outer function before plugging in complex values from the inner function.

71. Correct Answer: 18

The problem asks for the greatest integer value of a such that the **quadratic equation** has **two distinct real solutions**. First, rewrite the equation in **standard form**:

$$x(ax - 30) = -12$$

$$ax^2 - 30x = -12$$

$$ax^2 - 30x + 12 = 0$$

For a quadratic equation to have **two distinct real solutions**, the **discriminant** ($b^2 - 4ac$) must be greater than zero. Identify each part of the discriminant and then solve:

$$ax^2 - 30x + 12 = 0: a = a, -30 = b, 12 = c$$

$(-30)^2 - 4a(12) > 0$	Plug in
$900 - 48a > 0$	Multiply
$900 > 48a$	Add
$18.75 > a$	Divide

The question specifies that a is an integer constant. The largest integer less than 18.75 is 18.

Things to Remember:

- The discriminant ($b^2 - 4ac$) determines the number of solutions: $D > 0$ (2 real), $D = 0$ (1 real), $D < 0$ (no real solutions).

Vertex Form Equation of a Parabola

72. Correct Answer: A. $386 - 3(\frac{48}{6})^2$

The goal is to find an expression representing the maximum value of $q(x)$, where:

$$q(x) = p(x) + 2 = 48x - 3x^2 + 2.$$

Since $q(x) = -3x^2 + 48x + 2$ is a **quadratic function** with a negative leading coefficient, the **parabola** opens downward and has a maximum at its **vertex**.

The x–coordinate of the vertex is found using $x = \frac{-b}{2a}$:

$$x = \frac{-48}{(2(-3)} = \frac{48}{6}$$

To find the maximum value, substitute $x = \frac{48}{6}$ into $q(x)$:

$$q(x) = -3(\frac{48}{6})^2 + 48(\frac{48}{6}) + 2$$

$$q(x) = -3(\frac{48}{6})^2 + 386$$

This matches choice A.

Things to Remember:

- For a quadratic function $f(x) = ax^2 + bx + c$, the vertex occurs at $x = \frac{-b}{2a}$.
- When $a < 0$, the parabola opens downward and the vertex represents the maximum value.
- The maximum value can be expressed by substituting the vertex x–coordinate back into the function.

73. Correct Answer: B. $\frac{5}{3}$

The problem provides a system of equations consisting of a **quadratic** and a **linear** equation and states the graphs intersect at exactly one point, which means the system has only **one real solution.**

Set the two equations equal to each other to find the intersection points:

$$-3x^2 + 12x + 5 = 2x + b$$

Rearrange the equation into **standard quadratic** form by moving all terms to one side:

$$-3x^2 + 12x + 5 = 2x + b$$

$$0 = 3x^2 - 10x + 5 + b$$

When a quadratic equation has exactly one solution, it means the **discriminant** is zero, and the solution occurs at the **x-coordinate** of the **vertex.** The formula for the x–coordinate of the vertex is $x = \frac{-b}{2a}$. The coefficients from the equation are $a = 3$ and $b = -10$. Plug these into the vertex formula:

$x = \frac{-b}{2a}$

$x = \frac{-(-10)}{(2(3)}$ Plug-in

$x = \frac{10}{6} = \frac{5}{3}$ Simplify

Things to Remember:

- In a system of a parabola and a line, "exactly one point" of intersection usually refers to the vertex.
- The x–coordinate of the vertex for any quadratic is always $x = \frac{-b}{2a}$.

74. Correct Answer: D. 7

This is a rational equation. To solve it, we must find a common denominator for all terms.

First, factor the denominator on the right side of the equation:

$$x^2 - 2x - 8 = (x - 4)(x + 2)$$

Multiply both sides of the equation by $(x + 2)(x - 4)$ to clear the denominators:

$$\left(\frac{1}{x+2} + \frac{1}{x-4} = \frac{12}{(x-4)(x+2)}\right)(x-4)(x+2) \rightarrow (x-4) + (x+2) = 12$$

Combine like terms and solve for x:

$(x - 4) + (x + 2) = 12$	
$2x - 2 = 12$	Simplify
$2x = 14$	Add
$x = 7$	Divide

Things to Remember:

- Factor denominators first to identify the least common denominator (LCD).
- Once all terms have the same denominator, you can solve the resulting equation using only the numerators.

75. Correct Answer: $\frac{119}{3}$

The goal is to find the value of a, given that $x = 15$ is a solution to the equation. To do this, first factor the equation:

$$x(8x - 3a) + b(8x - 3a) - (x + b) = 0$$

$$(8x - 3a)(x + b) - (x + b) = 0$$

Now $(x + b)$ is common to both terms, so factor again:

$$(x + b)(8x - 3a - 1) = 0$$

This gives two possible solutions:

$$x = -b \text{ or } 8x - 3a - 1 = 0$$

Since b is a positive constant, $x = -b$ would be negative. Because $x = 15$ is positive, it must come from the second factor. Set the factor equal t0 zero and substitute $x = 15$:

$$8x - 3a - 1 = 0$$

$8(15) - 3a - 1 = 0$	Plug-in
$120 - 3a - 1 = 0$	Multiply
$119 = 3a$	Simplify
$a = \frac{119}{3}$	Divide

Things to Remember:

- Look for common factors that can be grouped together when factoring polynomials.
- When an equation factors into multiple parts, each factor set equal to zero provides a potential solution.

ADVANCED MATH

76 EQUIVALENT EXPRESSIONS

If $\frac{p}{q} = 45$ and $\frac{180p}{15yq} = 45$, what is the value of y?

A. $\frac{1}{12}$

B. $\frac{3}{5}$

C. 12

D. 15

77 EQUIVALENT EXPRESSIONS

$$\frac{2}{(x-2)\,(x+2)} = \frac{5}{10x}$$

Which value is a solution to the given equation?

A. $\frac{1}{2}$

B. $\frac{5}{2}$

C. 2

D. 4

78 EQUIVALENT EXPRESSIONS

$$\frac{36}{a} = \frac{36}{b} + \frac{36}{c} + \frac{36}{d}$$

The given equation relates the positive variables a, b, c, and d. Which of the following is equivalent to b?

A. $a + b + c$

B. $36(a + b + c)$

C. $\frac{acd}{cd - ad - ac}$

D. $\frac{36acd}{36(c + d) - 36a}$

79 EQUIVALENT EXPRESSIONS

The linear function h is defined by the function $h(x) = mx - 12x$, where m is a constant. If $h(c - 4) = \frac{3c}{2}$ where c is a constant and $c \neq 4$, which of the following expressions represents the value of m?

A. $\frac{15c}{2(c-4)}$

B. $\frac{3c}{2(c-4)} + 12$

C. $\frac{3c}{2c+8} + 12$

D. $\frac{9c}{2} - 48$

CONTINUE

ADVANCED MATH

80 EQUIVALENT EXPRESSIONS

If $15 + \frac{6(5-x)}{4} = \frac{9(5-x)}{2}$, which equation must also be true?

A. $5 - x = 5$

B. $x - 5 = 5$

C. $5 - x = -18$

D. $x - 5 = -18$

81 EQUIVALENT EXPRESSIONS

If m and p are numbers greater than 1 and $\sqrt[4]{m^3} = \sqrt[6]{p^2}$, for what value of a is $m^{3a-2} = p$?

82 EQUIVALENT EXPRESSIONS

Which expression is equivalent to $\frac{x+3}{x^2-5x+6} + \frac{2x-1}{x^2-9}$?

A. $\frac{3x^2-5x-15}{x^3-14x^2+45x-18}$

B. $\frac{x^2+2x-21}{(x-2)(x-3)(x-9)}$

C. $\frac{3x^2+10x+15}{(x-2)(x-3)(x+3)}$

D. $\frac{3x^2+x+11}{(x-2)(x-3)(x+3)}$

83 EQUIVALENT EXPRESSIONS

If $b > 0, x^2 + y^2 = 4b$ and $xy = 6 - b$, what is $(x + y)^2$ in terms of b?

A. $2b + 12$

B. $3b + 12$

C. $2b + 6$

D. $3b + 6$

CONTINUE

ADVANCED MATH

84

$$-\frac{3}{2}(6x-4)^2+\frac{5}{3}(6x-1)$$

The given expression can be written as a quadratic in the form ax^2+bx+c, where a, b, and c are constants. What is the value of $a+b+c$?

A. $-\frac{91}{3}$

B. $-\frac{7}{3}$

C. $\frac{7}{3}$

D. $\frac{161}{3}$

85 EQUIVALENT EXPRESSIONS

$$x^2+ax-84=(x+m)(x-n)$$

In the above expression, a, m, and n are integers. Which of the following must be true?

A. a is a factor of 3

B. n is a factor of 84

C. m is a factor of d

D. a is a factor of 84

86 EQUIVALENT EXPRESSIONS

The equation below relates distinct positive real numbers a, b, and c.

$$a = 9b^3\sqrt{(\frac{c}{3})^2}$$

Which equation correctly expresses c in terms of a and b?

A. $3\left(\frac{a}{9b}\right)^{\frac{2}{3}}$

B. $3\left(\frac{a}{9b}\right)^{\frac{3}{2}}$

C. $\left(\frac{a}{9b}\right)^{\frac{2}{3}}$

D. $27\left(\frac{a}{9b}\right)^{\frac{3}{2}}$

SEE SOLUTIONS ON NEXT PAGE

ANSWER KEY

QUESTIONS 61-75	
76	C
77	D
78	C
79	B
80	A
81	17/12
82	D
83	A
84	C
85	B
86	B

Don't just check the answer—master the method.
Get specific Desmos tips for each solution online. Gain access to The Gauntlet Mock Test and track your progress in real-time at **passthegauntlet.com.** Use code **GAUNTLETMATH20** to unlock 20% off your digital dashboard.

76. Correct Answer: C. 12

The problem provides two equations and asks for the value of y. Use substitution to simplify the second equation based on the information from the first. Notice that the second equation contains the ratio $\frac{p}{q}$, so rewrite it as:

$$\frac{180}{15y} \times \frac{p}{q} = 45$$

Substitute 45 for $\frac{p}{q}$ into this equation:

$$\frac{180}{15y} \times 45 = 45$$

Simplify to solve for y:

$\frac{180}{15y} \times 45 = 45$	
$\frac{180}{15y} = 1$	Divide
$180 = 15y$	Multiply
$y = 12$	Divide

Things to Remember:

- When comparing two expressions, find what they have in common and use substitution to solve.

Solve for Solution

77. Correct Answer: D. 4

To find the solution to this rational equation, use cross-multiplication to clear the denominators:

$$\frac{2}{(x-2)(x+4)} = \frac{5}{10x}$$

$2(10x) = 5(x-2)(x+4)$	Cross multiply
$2(10x) = 5(x^2 - 2x - 8)$	FOIL
$20x = 5x^2 - 10x - 40$	Distribute
$0 = 5x^2 - 30x - 40$	Simplify

Factor the expression to determine the solutions:

$0 = 5x^2 - 30x - 40$

$0 = 5(x^2 - 6x - 8)$

$0 = 5(x - 4)(x + 2)$

Set each factor equal to 0 to solve:

$$x - 4 = 0 \rightarrow x = 4$$

$$x + 2 = 0 \rightarrow x = -2$$

Of the given options, $x = 4$ matches with Choice D.

Things to Remember:

- Cross–multiplication is a fast way to solve equations where two fractions are set equal to each other.
- After finding solutions for a rational equation, check if they make any original denominator zero (extraneous solutions).

78. Correct Answer: C. $\frac{acd}{cd - ad - ac}$

This question requires isolating the variable b from an equation where all variables are in the denominators. Start by simplifying the given equation by dividing everything by 36:

$$\left(\frac{36}{a} = \frac{36}{b} + \frac{36}{c} + \frac{36}{d}\right) \div 36 \rightarrow \frac{1}{a} = \frac{1}{b} + \frac{1}{c} + \frac{1}{d}$$

Next, isolate the term containing b:

$$\frac{1}{a} = \frac{1}{b} + \frac{1}{c} + \frac{1}{d} \rightarrow \frac{1}{b} = \frac{1}{a} - \frac{1}{c} - \frac{1}{d}$$

Find a common denominator (acd) for the terms on the right side and then combine into a single fraction:

$$\frac{1}{b} = \frac{1}{a} - \frac{1}{c} - \frac{1}{d}$$

$$\frac{1}{b} = \frac{cd}{acd} - \frac{ad}{acd} - \frac{ac}{acd}$$ Rewrite with LCD

$$\frac{1}{b} = \frac{cd - ad - ac}{acd}$$ Combine

Take the reciprocal of both sides to get the final equation in terms of b:

$$b = \frac{acd}{cd - ad - ac}$$

Things to Remember:

- When isolating a variable in a denominator, first isolate the entire fractional term, then take the reciprocal at the very end.
- To subtract fractions with different variables as denominators, use the product of all those variables as your common denominator.

79. Correct Answer: B. $\frac{3c}{2(c-4)} + 12$

The problem asks for an expression for m given a **linear function** $h(x)$ and a specific output value. To solve, plug–in the given expression $h(c-4) = \frac{3c}{2}$ into $h(x)$:

$h(x) = mx - 12x$

$\frac{3c}{2} = m(c-4) - 12(c-4)$ Plug-in

Factor $(c-4)$ and then isolate m:

$\frac{3c}{2} = m(c-4) - 12(c-4)$

$\frac{3c}{2} = (m-12)(c-4)$ Factor

$\frac{3c}{2(c-4)} = m - 12$ Divide

$m = \frac{3c}{2(c-4)} + 12$ Add

Things to Remember:

- When given a function and an input, start by plugging-in and then isolating the missing term.

80. Correct Answer: A. $5 - x = 5$

To determine which equation must be true, solve the given equation for the value of x:

$$15 + \frac{6(5 - x)}{4} = \frac{9(5 - x)}{2}$$

$60 + 6(5 - x) = 18(5 - x)$	Multiply by 4
$60 + 30 - 6x = 90 - 18x$	Distribute
$90 - 6x = 90 - 18x$	Simplify
$12x = 0$	Combine like terms
$x = 0$	Divide

Plug-in this solution into each answer to determine which one holds true. Plugging in $x = 0$ into Choice A gives:

$$5 - x = 5 \rightarrow 5 - 0 = 5 \rightarrow 5 = 5$$

Since $x = 0$ makes Choice A true, it is the correct answer.

Things to Remember:

- Clearing denominators by multiplying by the Least Common Multiple (LCM) simplifies complex rational equations.
- If an equation is true, the value of the variable must satisfy any other derived or equivalent equation.

CONTINUE

81. Correct Answer: $\frac{17}{12}$

The problem requires solving for the value of the constant a by relating two equations involving *m* and *p*. Start by converting the radicals in the first equation to fractional exponents:

$$\sqrt[4]{m^3} = m^{\frac{3}{4}}$$
$$\sqrt[6]{p^2} = p^{\frac{2}{6}} = p^{\frac{1}{3}}$$

Simplify the given relationship using these fractional exponent terms:

$\sqrt[4]{m^3} = \sqrt[6]{p^2} \rightarrow m^{\frac{3}{4}} = p^{\frac{1}{3}}$

$(m^{\frac{3}{4}})^3 = (p^{\frac{1}{3}})^3$

$m^{\frac{9}{4}} = p$

Now find the value of a based on the given relationship. Exponential expressions with the same base on either side of the equal sign have equivalent exponents:

$m^{3a-2} = p$	
$m^{3a-2} = m^{\frac{9}{4}}$	Substitute
$3a - 2 = \frac{9}{4}$	Set exponents equal
$3a = \frac{17}{4}$	Add
$a = \frac{17}{12}$	Divide

Things to Remember:

- Radical expressions can be rewritten as rational exponents to make them easier to manipu late algebraically.
- When the bases of two equal exponential expressions are the same, their exponents must also be equal.

CONTINUE

Simplify Expression

82. Correct Answer: D. $\frac{3x^2 + x + 11}{(x-2)(x-3)(x+3)}$

To find the equivalent expression, add the two rational expressions by finding a common denominator. To do this, first factor the denominators of both expressions:

$$x^2 - 5x + 66 \rightarrow (x-2)(x-3)$$

$$x^2 - 9 \rightarrow (x-3)(x+3)$$

Identify the Least Common Denominator (LCD), which must include all unique factors from both denominators:

$$\text{LCD} = (x-2)(x-3)(x+3)$$

Rewrite each fraction with the common denominator by multiplying by the "missing" factor:

$$\frac{x+3}{x^2 - 5x + 6} \rightarrow \frac{x+3}{(x-2)(x-3)} \times \frac{x+3}{x+3} = \frac{(x+3)(x+3)}{(x-2)(x-3)(x+3)}$$

$$\frac{2x-1}{x^2-9} \rightarrow \frac{2x-1}{(x+3)(x-3)} \times \frac{x-2}{x-2} = \frac{(2x-1)(x-2)}{(x-2)(x-3)(x+3)}$$

Expand the numerators and then combine like terms to simplify:

$$\frac{(x+3)(x+3)}{(x-2)(x-3)(x+3)} + \frac{(2x-1)(x-2)}{(x-2)(x-3)(x+3)}$$

$$\frac{(x^2 + 6x + 9)}{(x-2)(x-3)(x+3)} + \frac{(2x^2 - 5x + 2)}{(x-2)(x-3)(x+3)} \quad \text{Expand numerators}$$

$$\frac{3x^2 + x + 11}{(x-2)(x-3)(x+3)} \quad \text{Simplify}$$

Things to Remember:

- Factoring denominators is the essential first step for adding or subtracting rational expressions.
- Always multiply the numerator and denominator by the same factor to maintain the value of the fraction.

CONTINUE

83. Correct Answer: A. $2b + 12$

When given multiple expressions, evaluate one in terms of the other. Start by expanding the squared binomial:

$$(x + y)^2 \rightarrow x^2 + 2xy + y^2$$

The question states $x^2 + y^2 = 4b$ and $xy = 6 - b$. Rearrange the expression and substitute the given values to rewrite everything in terms of b:

$x^2 + 2xy + y^2 \rightarrow x^2 + y^2 + 2xy$	Rearrange
$4b + 2(6 - b)$	Substitute
$4b + 12 - 2b$	Distribute
$2b + 12$	Simplify

Therefore, the given expression simplifies to $2b + 12$.

Things to Remember:

- Recognizing algebraic patterns like $(x + y)^2 \rightarrow x^2 + 2xy + y^2$ allows for quick substitution in system-style problems.

84. Correct Answer: C. $\frac{7}{3}$

To find the value of $a + b + c$, we must first rewrite the given expression in the standard quadratic form $ax^2 + bx + c$.

$-\frac{3}{2}(6x - 4)^2 + \frac{5}{3}(6x - 1)$

$-\frac{3}{2}(36x^2 - 48x + 16) + \frac{5}{3}(6x - 1)$ Expand

$-54x^2 + 72x - 24 + 10x - \frac{5}{3}$ Distribute

$-54x^2 + 82x - \frac{77}{3}$ Simplify

Identify each part of the expression to determine the value of a, b, and c.

$$-54x^2 + 82x - \frac{77}{3} = ax^2 + bx + c$$

Therefore, $a = -54$, $b = 82$, and $c = -\frac{77}{3}$. Add $a + b + c$ to find the final result:

$$a + b + c = -54 + 82 - \frac{77}{3} = \frac{7}{3}$$

Things to Remember:

- Standard form for a quadratic is $ax^2 + bx + c$.
- To solve for missing constants, set equivalent expressions equal to each other and simplify.

CONTINUE

SOLUTIONS
EQUIVALENT EXPRESSIONS

Simplify Expression

85. Correct Answer: B. *n* is a factor of 84

This problem involves matching coefficients and constants between equivalent forms of a **quadratic** expression. Simplify and compare both sides of the equation to evaluate each answer choice:

$$x^2 + dx - 84 = (x + m)(x - n)$$

$$x^2 + dx - 84 = x^2 + mx - nx - mn$$

The following parts of the equation can be set equivalent:

$$x^2 = x^2$$

$$dx = mx - nx$$

$$-84 = -mn$$

Since m and n are integers and their product is 84, n must be a factor of 84.

Things to Remember:

- When a quadratic is factored, the product of the constants in the factors equals the constant term of the original quadratic.
- If the product of two integers equals a specific value, those integers are factors of that value.

86. Correct Answer: B. $3(\frac{a}{9b})^{\frac{3}{2}}$

The goal is to isolate the variable c from the equation $a = 9b^3 \sqrt{(\frac{c}{3})^2}$ by moving over each term one at a time:

$a = 9b^3 \sqrt{(\frac{c}{3})^2}$

$\frac{a}{9b} = \sqrt[3]{(\frac{c}{3})^2}$ — Divide by $9b$

$\frac{a^3}{9b} = (\frac{c}{3})^2$ — Cube both sides

$(\frac{a}{9b})^{\frac{3}{2}} = (\frac{c}{3})$ — Take the square root

$c = 3(\frac{a}{9b})^{\frac{3}{2}}$ — Multiply by 3

The final expression in terms of c can be written as $3(\frac{a}{9b})^{\frac{3}{2}}$.

Things to Remember:

- Radicals can be rewritten as rational exponents using the rule: $\sqrt[n]{x^m} = x^{\frac{m}{n}}$.
- When isolating variables, apply operations in the reverse order of operations.

87 RATIOS, RATES, PROPORTIONS, AND UNITS

A pump fills a tank at a rate of 45,000 cubic inches per hour. Which of the following is closest to this rate in liters per minute? (Use 1 inch = 2.54 centimeters and 1 liter = 1000 cubic centimeters)

A. 1.91

B. 4.84

C. 12.29

D. 122.9

88 RATIOS, RATES, PROPORTIONS, AND UNITS

A storage tank has a volume of 0.62 cubic meters. Which of the following is closest to this volume in gallons? (Use 1 meter = 100 centimeters, 1 inch = 2.54 centimeters, and 1 gallon = 231 cubic inches)

A. 16.38

B. 163.79

C. 620.00

D. 1056.69

89 RATIOS, RATES, PROPORTIONS, AND UNITS

The ratio of a flag's length to its width is 9 to 5. If the width of the flag is increased by 8 units, how must the length change to maintain this ratio?

A. It must decrease by 8 units.

B. It must increase by 8 units.

C. It must increase by 14.4 units.

D. It must decrease by 14.4 units.

90 RATIOS, RATES, PROPORTIONS, AND UNITS

An architect makes two scale drawings of a new rectangular billboard. In both drawings, the ratio of length to width is 15:6. In the second drawing, the width is made 3.5 times as large as the width in the first drawing so the details are easier to see. How does the length of the second drawing compare to the length of the first drawing?

A. The length of the second drawing is 0.286 times the length of the first drawing.

B. The length of the second drawing is 2.5 times the length of the first drawing.

C. The length of the second drawing is 8.75 times the length of the first drawing.

D. The length of the second drawing is 3.5 times the length of the first drawing.

CONTINUE

PROBLEM SOLVING AND DATA ANALYSIS

91 RATIOS, RATES, PROPORTIONS, AND UNITS

One bucket of waterproofing costs $18 and covers 160 square feet of surface. A roof deck has a total area of w square feet and must be sealed four times. Which equation represents the cost c, in dollars, of the waterproofing needed?

A. $c = \dfrac{18w}{40}$

B. $c = \dfrac{18(4w)}{40}$

C. $c = \dfrac{40w}{18}$

D. $c = \dfrac{320w}{5}$

92 RATIOS, RATES, PROPORTIONS, AND UNITS

The density of a certain metal is 1100 kilograms per cubic meter. A solid sphere of this metal has a diameter of 0.6 meters. To the nearest whole number, what is the mass, in kilograms, of the sphere?

A. 62

B. 124

C. 207

D. 412

ANSWER KEY

QUESTIONS 87-92	
87	C
88	B
89	C
90	D
91	A
92	B

Don't just check the answer—master the method.
Get specific Desmos tips for each solution online. Gain access to The Gauntlet Mock Test and track your progress in real-time at **passthegauntlet.com.** Use code **GAUNTLETMATH20** to unlock 20% off your digital dashboard.

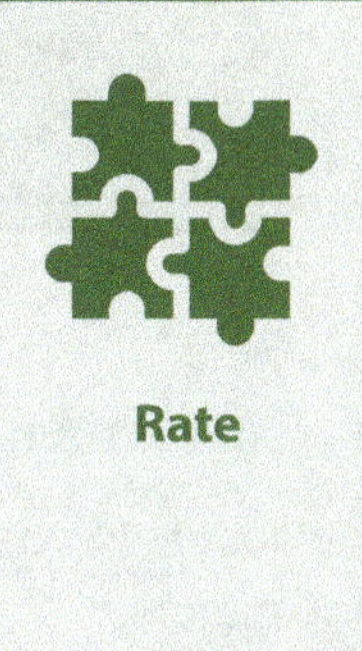

87. Correct Answer: C. 12.29

The problem asks for a rate conversion from cubic inches per hour to liters per minute. This requires a multi-step process using **dimensional analysis**. First, convert cubic inches to cubic centimeters:

$$1 \text{ inch} = 2.54 \text{ centimeters}$$

$$1 \text{ cubic inch} = 2.54^3 \text{ cubic centimeters}$$

$$1 \text{ cubic inch} \approx 16.387064 \text{ cubic centimeters}$$

Then multiply by this conversion rate to go from cubic inches per hour to cubic centimeters per hour:

$$45{,}000 \times 16.387064 \approx 737{,}417.88 \text{ cubic centimeters per hour}$$

Next, convert cubic centimeters to liters using 1 liter = 1000 cubic centimeters:

$$\frac{737{,}417.88}{1000} \approx 737.41788 \text{ liters per hour}$$

Finally, convert the time from hours to minutes. Since there are 60 minutes in 1 hour, divide the hourly rate by 60:

$$\frac{737.41788}{60} \approx 12.29$$

The value closest to this result is 12.29.

Things to Remember:

- When converting volume units, remember to cube the linear conversion factor (e.g., if 1 inch = 2.54 cm, then 1 cubic inch = 16.387 cubic cm).
- Pay close attention to the time units (hours to minutes) to ensure you are multiplying or dividing correctly based on the rate.

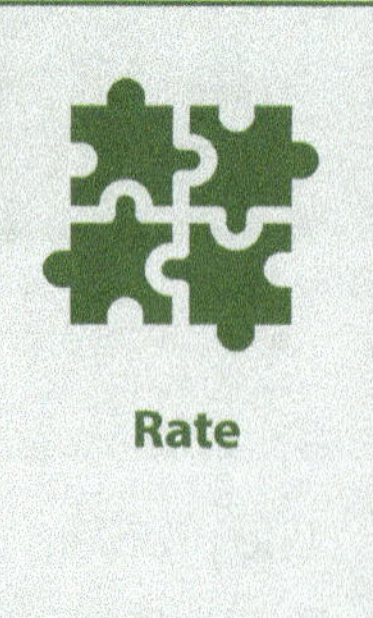

88. Correct Answer: B. 163.79

The goal is to convert 0.62 cubic meters into gallons. First, convert cubic meters to cubic centimeters:

$$1 \text{ meter} = 100 \text{ centimeters}$$

$$1 \text{ cubic meter} = 100^3 \text{ cubic centimeters}$$

$$1 \text{ cubic meter} = 1{,}000{,}000 \text{ cubic centimeters}$$

$$0.62 \times 1{,}000{,}000 = 620{,}000 \text{ cubic centimeters}$$

Next, convert these cubic centimeters into cubic inches:

$$1 \text{ inch} = 2.54 \text{ centimeters}$$

$$1 \text{ cubic inch} = 2.54^3 \text{ cubic centimeters}$$

$$1 \text{ cubic inch} \approx 16.387064 \text{ cubic centimeters}$$

$$\frac{620{,}000}{16.387064} \approx 37{,}834.72 \text{ cubic inches}$$

Finally, convert cubic inches to gallons using the provided conversion:

$$1 \text{ gallon} = 231 \text{ cubic inches}$$

$$\frac{37{,}834.72}{231} \approx 163.786 \text{ gallons}$$

Rounding to the hundredths place gives 163.79.

Things to Remember:

- To convert from a metric unit to a standard unit, ensure you are using the cubed version of the linear conversion for volume.

89. Correct Answer: C. 14.4

The original ratio of length to width is 9 to 5. To evaluate the change, represent the original dimensions as $9k$ and $5k$, where k is a constant. The problem states the width is increased by 8 units. The new width is therefore $(5k + 8)$.

To maintain the 9:5 ratio, the new length must be $\frac{9}{5}$ times the new width:

$$\frac{9}{5}(5k + 8)$$

To determine the change in length, distribute and compare to the original length of $9k$:

$\frac{9}{5}(5k + 8)$	
$\frac{9}{5}(5k) + \frac{9}{5}(8)$	Distribute
$9k + 14.4$	Simplify

Comparing this to 9k shows an increase of 14.4 units.

Note: You can also solve this by picking a "test" width. If the original width is 5, the length is 9. If you increase the width by 8, the new width is 13. Set up a proportion: 9 / 5 = x / 13. Cross-multiply: 5x = 117. Solve for x: x = 23.4. The increase is 23.4 - 9 = 14.4.

Things to Remember:

- Proportions can be solved by setting up two equivalent fractions and cross-multiplying.
- When a dimension is "increased by" a value, use addition; when it is "increased by a factor," use multiplication.

90. Correct Answer: D. The length of the second drawing is 3.5 times the length of the first drawing.

In the second drawing, the width is made 3.5 times as large as the width in the first drawing. Because the two drawings are **proportional** (they share the same length-to-width ratio), any scale factor applied to the width must also apply to the length to keep the ratio constant.

Things to Remember:

- In similar figures or scale drawings, all corresponding linear dimensions (length, width, perimeter, etc.) change by the same scale factor.

91. Correct Answer: A. $c = \frac{18w}{40}$

To find an equation that represents the total cost (c) to seal a roof deck, first determine the total surface area to be covered and then calculate how many buckets of waterproofing are needed to cover that area.

The roof deck has an area of w square feet, but because it must be sealed four times, the total area to be covered is $4w$ square feet.

Next, determine the number of buckets needed. Since one bucket covers 160 square feet, we divide the total coverage area by the coverage per bucket:

$$\frac{4w}{160} = \frac{w}{40}$$

Finally, calculate the total cost (c) by multiplying the number of buckets by the price per bucket ($18):

$$c = 18 \times \frac{w}{40} = \frac{18w}{40}$$

Things to Remember:

- Always simplify intermediate fractions to see if they match the structure of the provided answer choices.

CONTINUE

92. Correct Answer: B. 124

To find the mass of the sphere, we must first calculate its volume and then use the given density. The relationship between these is defined by the formula:

$$\text{Mass} = \text{Density} \times \text{Volume}$$

First, calculate the volume of the solid sphere. The problem provides a diameter of 0.6 meters, which means the radius (r) is 0.3 meters. Substitute the radius into the formula:

$$V = \frac{4}{3}\pi r^3$$

$$V = \frac{4}{3}\pi(0.3)^3 \approx 0.1131\ m3$$

Now the density to find the mass. Use the given density of 1100 kilograms per cubic meter.

$$\text{Mass} = 1100 \times 0.1131 = 124.41 \text{ kg}$$

To the nearest whole number, the mass is 124 kg.

Things to Remember:

- Always verify if you are given the diameter or the radius to avoid common math errors. Density is equal to the mass divided by volume.

93 PERCENTAGES

$$0.12x + 0.30y = 0.24(x + y)$$

The equation models mixing x gallons of a 12% solution with y gallons of a 30% solution to obtain a 24% solution. If 80 gallons of the 12% solution are used, how many gallons of the 30% solution are needed?

A. 24

B. 80

C. 120

D. 160

94 PERCENTAGES

For the positive quantities p, q, and r, 18% of p is equivalent to 12% of q, and q is equivalent to 60% of r. What percentage of r is p? (Disregard the % sign when entering your answer.)

95 PERCENTAGES

The positive number a is 1,764% of the sum of the positive numbers b and c, and b is 75% of c. What percent of b is a?

A. 1116%

B. 2,352%

C. 3,087%

D. 4,116%

96 PERCENTAGES

In 2015, a company employed 48 workers, each classified as either part-time or full-time. From 2015 to 2025, the number of part-time workers increased by approximately 37%, and the number of full-time workers increased by approximately 62%. The total workforce increased by approximately 49%. Which equation best represents this situation, where x is the number of part-time workers in 2015 and y is the number of full-time workers in 2015?

A. $1.62x + 1.37y = 48(1.49)$

B. $1.37x + 1.49y = 48(1.62)$

C. $1.37x + 1.62y = 48(1.49)$

D. $1.49x + 1.49y = 48(1.49)$

PROBLEM SOLVING AND DATA ANALYSIS

97 PERCENTAGES

A horticulturist mixes p liters of a 10% fertilizer solution with q liters of a 25% fertilizer solution to obtain a 20% fertilizer solution. Which equation best represents this situation?

A. $0.10p + 0.25q = 20(p + q)$

B. $0.10p + 0.25q = 0.20(p + q)$

C. $10p + 25q = 0.20(p + q)$

D. $0.1p + 2.5q = 20(p + q)$

98 PERCENTAGES

The price of item A is 372% of the price of item B, and the price of item A is 0.062% of the price of item C. If the price of item C is p% of the price of item B, what is the value of ?

99 PERCENTAGES

The function $f(n) = 3(10.2)^{\frac{n-2}{5}}$ gives each term of a sequence as a function of the position n, where n is a whole number. The value of the term in position 17 is p% more than the value of the term in position 7. What is the value of p?

100 PERCENTAGES

The positive number a is 3,120% of the number c, and c is 16% of the number b. What is the value of a–b in terms of c?

A. 24.95c

B. 31.04c

C. 31.14c

D. 3113.75c

101 PERCENTAGES

A company tracked two products, Product X and Product Y. At the beginning of the year, sales of the two products were equal. By the end of the year, sales of Product X had increased by 2,400% of its starting value, and sales of Product Y had increased by 150% of its starting value. At the end of the year, sales of Product X were $p\%$ greater than sales of Product Y. What is the value of p?

ANSWER KEY

QUESTIONS 93-101	
93	D
94	40
95	D
96	C
97	B
98	600,000
99	10304
100	A
101	900

Don't just check the answer—master the method.
Get specific Desmos tips for each solution online. Gain access to The Gauntlet Mock Test and track your progress in real-time at **passthegauntlet.com.** Use code **GAUNTLETMATH20** to unlock 20% off your digital dashboard.

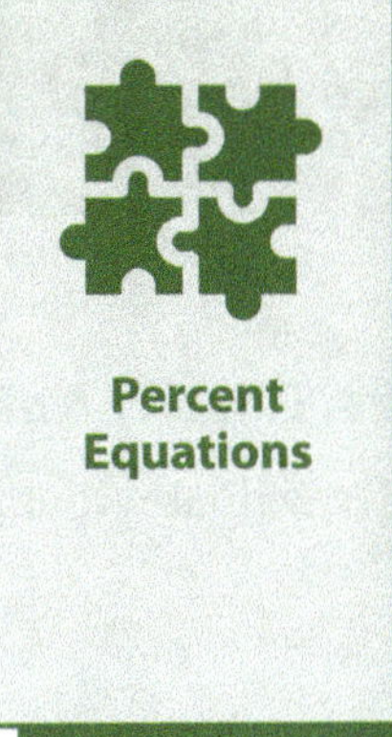

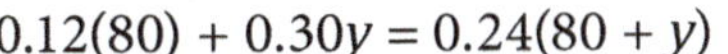

93. Correct Answer: D. 160

The problem provides a **linear equation** that models mixing two different solutions to achieve a specific concentration: $0.12x + 0.30y = 0.24(x + y)$. In this model, x represents the gallons of the 12% solution, and y represents the gallons of the 30% solution.

The problem states that 80 gallons of the 12% solution are used, so start by substituting $x = 80$ into the given expression. Then solve for y:

$0.12(80) + 0.30y = 0.24(80 + y)$	Substitute
$9.6 + 0.30y = 19.2 + 0.24y$	Distribute
$0.06y = 9.6$	Combine like terms
$y = 160$	Divide

This means 160 gallons of the 30% solution are needed.

Things to Remember:

- When solving mixture problems, the decimal coefficients represent the percentage concentration of the substance.

A Number Percent of Another Number

94. Correct Answer: 40

To evaluate what percent p is of r, translate the given information into mathematical expressions:

$$18\% \text{ of } p \text{ is equivalent to } 12\% \text{ of } q \rightarrow 0.18p = 0.12q$$

$$q \text{ is equivalent to } 60\% \text{ of } r \rightarrow q = 0.60r$$

Combine the expressions to determine the relationship between p and r. Then simplify:

$0.18p = 0.12(0.60r)$

$0.18p = 0.072r$	Simplify
$p = 0.40r$	Divide

Converting the decimal 0.40 into a percentage shows that p is 40% of r.

Things to Remember:

- To compare two variables that aren't directly linked, express both in terms of a common third variable.
- When the question asks for a percentage and tells you to disregard the % sign, provide the numerical value rather than the decimal.

95. Correct Answer: D. 4,116%

This problem requires manipulating multiple percentage relationships to find how a relates to b. First, rewrite each relationship as an expression:

a is 1,764% of the sum of b and $c \rightarrow a = 17.64(b + c)$

b is 75% of $c \rightarrow b = 0.75c$

Next, rewrite the second expression to solve for c in terms of b:

$$b = 0.75c$$

$$c = \frac{b}{0.75}$$

Now substitute this into the first expression to evaluate the what percent a is of b:

$a = 17.64(b + \frac{b}{0.75})$	Substitute
$a = 17.64b + 23.52b$	Distribute
$a = 41.16b$	Simplify

Convert the decimal to a percentage to match to Choice D.

$41.16 \times 100 = 4116\%$

Things to Remember:

- Percentages greater than 100% are represented by decimals greater than 1.

CONTINUE

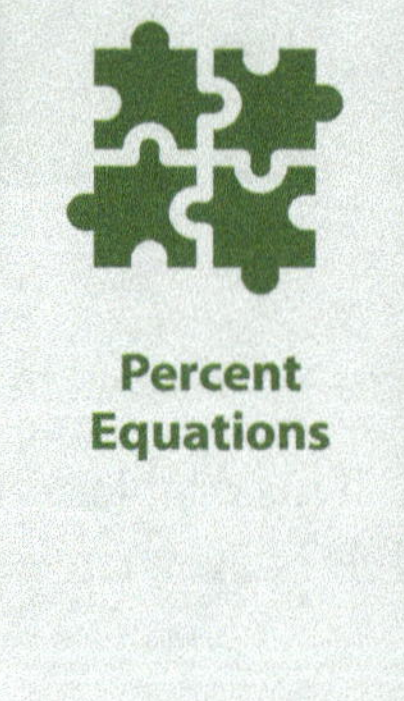

96. Correct Answer: C. $1.37x + 1.62y = 48(1.49)$

The goal is to find the equation that represents the total workforce in 2025 based on growth rates since 2015.

First, translate the individual growth rates into multipliers:

- Part-time workers (x) increased by 37% → $1.37x$
- Full-time workers (y) increased by 62% → $1.62y$

Next, express the total workforce in 2025. In 2015, the total was 48 workers. Since the total workforce increased by 49%, the new total is 48 multiplied by 1.49. Setting the sum of the new parts equal to the new total gives the equation:

$$1.37x + 1.62y = 48(1.49)$$

Things to Remember:

- A percentage increase is represented by $(1 + r)$, where r is the decimal form of the rate.

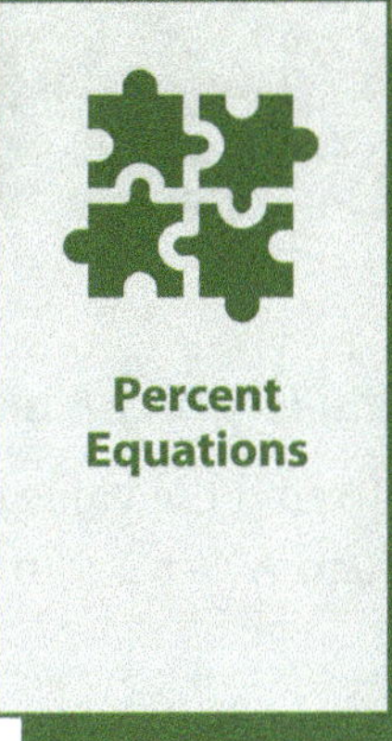

97. Correct Answer: B. $0.10p + 0.25q = 0.20(p + q)$

The problem requires an equation to model a **mixture** of two fertilizer solutions. The total amount of pure fertilizer in the final mixture must equal the sum of the pure fertilizer from each individual solution.

First, express the amount of fertilizer from each solution as a decimal multiplier:

p liters of 10% solution → $0.10p$

q liters of 25% solution → $0.25q$

The final mixture consists of the combined volume, which is $(p + q)$ liters. Since the goal is a 20% solution, the amount of fertilizer in the final mix is represented as:

$$0.20(p + q)$$

Setting the sum of the parts equal to the total gives the equation:

$$0.10p + 0.25q = 0.20(p + q)$$

Things to Remember:

- In mixture problems, the coefficients represent the concentration of the substance expressed as a decimal.
- The total volume of a mixture is the sum of the volumes of its individual components.

SOLUTIONS
PERCENTAGES

A Number Percent of Another Number

98. Correct Answer: 600,000

To find the value of p, first establish the relationship between the prices of items B and C by using item A as a common link. To do this, first translate the percentage relationships into equations:

$$\text{item A is 372\% of item B} \rightarrow A = 3.72B$$

$$\text{item A is 0.062\% of item C} \rightarrow A = 0.00062C$$

Next, set the two expressions for A equal to each other to find the relationship between B and C:

$$3.72B = 0.00062C$$

Divide by 0.00062 to isolate C:

$$C = 6{,}000B$$

The problem asks for the value of p, where the price of item C is *p*% of the price of item B:

$$C = \left(\frac{p}{100}\right) \times B \rightarrow 6{,}000B = \left(\frac{p}{100}\right) \times B$$

$$6{,}000 = \frac{p}{100}$$

$$p = 600{,}000$$

Things to Remember:

- When a question involves three variables, use the one common to both statements to link the other two.

99. Correct Answer: 10304

The problem involves comparing two terms in a sequence defined by an exponential function to find a percentage increase.

First, compute the values for position 17 and position 7:

$$f(17) = 3(10.2)^{\frac{17-2}{5}} = 3(10.2)^3$$

$$f(7) = 3(10.2)^{\frac{7-2}{5}} = 3(10.2)^1$$

Next, determine the ratio between the two terms:

$$\frac{f(17)}{f(7)} = \frac{3(10.2)^3}{3(10.2)^1} = (10.2)^2 = 104.04$$

To find what percent greater $f(17)$ is compared to $f(7)$, rewrite their ratio as a percentage:

$$f(17) = 104.04f(7) \rightarrow f(17)(1 + \frac{p}{100})f(7)$$

$$104.04 = 1 + \frac{p}{100}$$

$$103.04 = \frac{p}{100}$$

$$p = 10304$$

Things to Remember:

- When dividing terms with the same base, subtract the exponents.
- "Percent more" refers to the growth beyond 100%, so use percent increase to evaluate.

CONTINUE

SOLUTIONS
PERCENTAGES

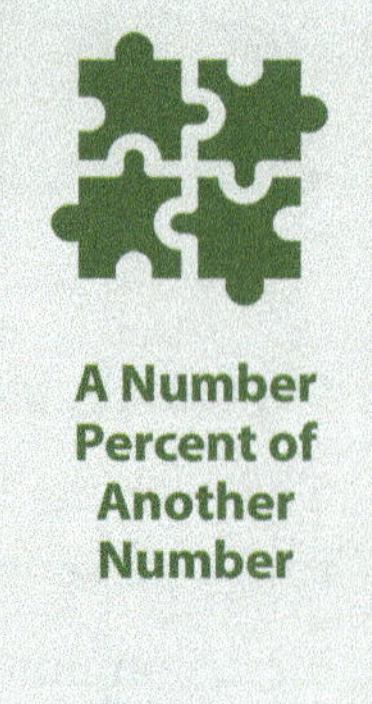

100. Correct Answer: A. $24.95c$

The goal is to express the value of $a - b$ entirely in terms of the variable c. Start by translating the percentage statements into algebraic equations:

$$a \text{ is } 3{,}120\% \text{ of } c \rightarrow a = 31.20c$$

$$c \text{ is } 16\% \text{ of } b \rightarrow c = 0.16b$$

Next, rewrite the second equation to solve for b in terms of c:

$$c = 0.16b \rightarrow b = \frac{c}{0.16} \rightarrow b = 6.25c$$

Now, substitute the expressions for a and b into the expression $a - b$:

$$a - b = 31.20c - 6.25c = 24.95c$$

Things to Remember:

- Percents can be turned into expressions by rewriting them as decimals.

The Original Number before a Percent Increase/ Decrease

101. Correct Answer: 900

To find the percentage by which sales of Product X are greater than sales of Product Y at the end of the year first define the starting values. Let S represent the starting sales for both products, since the problem states their sales were equal at the beginning of the year. Next, calculate the end-of-year sales for each product based on their respective percentage increases:

Product X → Sales increased by 2,400% of its starting value:

$$\text{Final Sales of X} = S + 24S = 25S$$

Product Y → Sales increased by 150% of its starting value:

$$\text{Final Sales of Y} = S + 1.5S = 2.5S$$

Now, compare the final values of the two products by finding their ratio:

$$\frac{\text{Final X}}{\text{Final Y}} = \frac{25S}{2.5S} = 10$$

This means the final sales of Product X are 10 times the final sales of Product Y. To find the percentage greater than (p), use the relationship:

$10 = 1 + \frac{p}{100}$

$9 = \frac{p}{100}$ Subtract

$p = 900$ Multiply

The value of Product X is 900% greater than Product Y.

Things to Remember:

- When a value is "increased by" a percentage, you must add that increase to the original 100%.
- "Percent greater than" measures the additional amount beyond the baseline.

PROBLEM SOLVING AND DATA ANALYSIS

101 ONE-VARIABLE DATA

Data set H consists of 41 integers, each between 300 and 500 inclusive. Data set J consists of the same 41 integers in H together with the integer 1000. Which of the following must be greater for data set J than for data set H?

I. The mean

II. The median

A. I only

B. II only

C. I and II

D. Neither I nor II

102 ONE-VARIABLE DATA

Data Set S	1	1	2	2	3	3
Data Set R	5	5	6	6	7	7

The standard deviation of data set S is s and the standard deviation of data set R is r. Which of the following statements is true?

A. $r < s$

B. $r > s$

C. $r = s$

D. The relationship cannot be determined

SEE SOLUTIONS ON NEXT PAGE

ANSWER KEY

QUESTIONS 102-103	
102	A
103	C

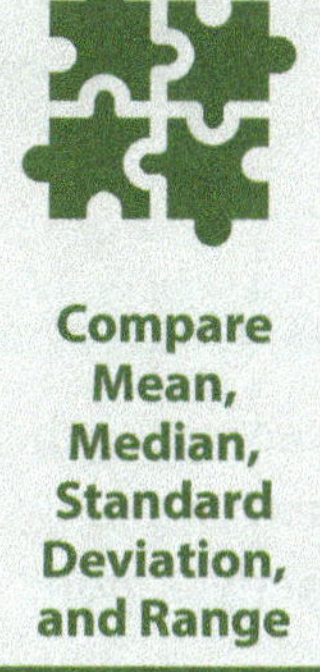

102. Correct Answer: A. I only

The goal of this problem is to determine how adding an extreme value (an outlier) to a data set affects the **mean** and the **median.** Data set H consists of 41 integers between 300 and 500. Data set J includes all those same integers plus the number 1000.

First, compare the means of the data sets. The **mean** is calculated by finding the average of all values in a set:

- Adding the integer 1000, which is significantly greater than any other number in the original set, will increase the sum of the values substantially.
- Because 1000 is greater than every number in data set H, its addition will pull the average (mean) upward.
- Therefore, the mean of data set J must be greater than the mean of data set H.

Next, compare the medians of the data sets. The **median** is the middle value of a data set when ordered from least to greatest:

- Data set H has 41 values, so the median is the 21st value.
- Data set J has 42 values, so the median is the average of the 21st and 22nd values.
- Since there are many integers in the set and they are all within a specific range (300 to 500), there is no guarantee that the median will change by adding one value at the end. For example, if many of the middle values are the same, the median might remain identical.

The final conclusion is that only the mean will be greater.

Things to Remember:

- The mean is highly sensitive to outliers. Adding a value much larger than the rest of the set will always increase the mean.
- The median is resistant to outliers. In a large data set, adding one extreme value at the end of the list rarely changes the middle value significantly.

SOLUTIONS
ONE-VARIABLE DATA

103. Correct Answer: C. $r = s$

To compare the **standard deviations** (s and r) of two provided data sets, evaluate the relationship between the two data sets: By comparing the numbers, you can see that each value in data set R is exactly 4 more than the corresponding value in data set S.

Next, evaluate the **standard deviation** based on the spread of the numbers:

- Standard deviation measures how spread out the numbers are from their mean.
- Because every number in the set was shifted by the same amount (+4), the distance between the numbers remains exactly the same.
- Since both data sets have the same "spread" or dispersion, their standard deviations must be equal.

Therefore, $r = s$.

Things to Remember:

- Adding or subtracting a constant value from every number in a data set does not change the standard deviation.
- Standard deviation is a measure of spread; if the relative distance between data points is preserved, the standard deviation remains constant.

104 TWO-VARIABLE DATA

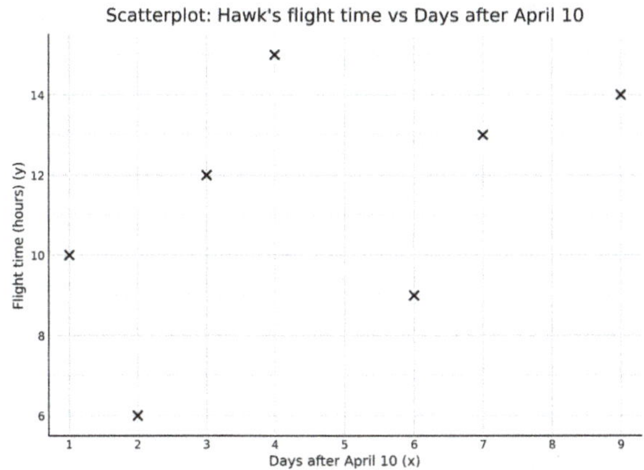

The scatterplot shows the relationship between the length of time y, in hours, a hawk spends in flight and x, the number of days after April 10. What is the average rate of change, in hours per day, of the hawk's flight time from April 12 to April 17?

ANSWER KEY

QUESTIONS 104	
104	1.4

104. Correct Answer: 1.4

The question asks for the average rate of change of the hawk's flight time between April 12 and April 17. In a graphical context, the **average rate of change** is equivalent to the **slope** between two points.

First, identify the x–values for the dates provided. Since x represents the number of days after April 10:

- April 12 is 2 days after April 10 ($x = 2$).
- April 17 is 7 days after April 10 ($x = 7$).

Next, locate these x-values on the scatterplot to find their corresponding y–values (flight time in hours): At $x = 2$, the data point is located at $y = 6$. This gives us the coordinate (2, 6). At $x = 7$, the data point is located at $y = 13$. This gives us the coordinate (7, 13).

To find the average rate of change, apply the slope formula:

$$\frac{\Delta y}{\Delta x} = \frac{(13 - 6)}{(7 - 2)} = \frac{7}{5} = 1.4$$

The average rate of change is 1.4 hours per day.

Note: You can also solve this by manually counting the "rise" and the "run" on the graph grid between the two points. Moving from (2, 6) to (7, 13) requires going up 7 units (rise) and right 5 units (run). Dividing the rise by the run (7/5) results in 1.4.

Things to Remember:

- Average rate of change is simply the slope between two points.

105 PROBABILITY

For the last 120 books checked out of the library, the table summarizes the distribution of classification and page count.

Classification	Page Count		
	200	200-350	>350
Fiction	28	18	8
Nonfiction	6	22	12
Reference	0	10	20

One book will be selected at random. What is the probability that the selected book has at most 350 pages, given that it is not classified in the Reference category? (Express your answer as a fraction or a decimal, not a percent.)

SEE SOLUTIONS ON NEXT PAGE

ANSWER KEY

QUESTIONS 105	
105	7/9 or 0.7777 or 0.7778

Don't just check the answer—master the method.
Get specific Desmos tips for each solution online. Gain access to The Gauntlet Mock Test and track your progress in real-time at **passthegauntlet.com.** Use code **GAUNTLETMATH20** to unlock 20% off your digital dashboard.

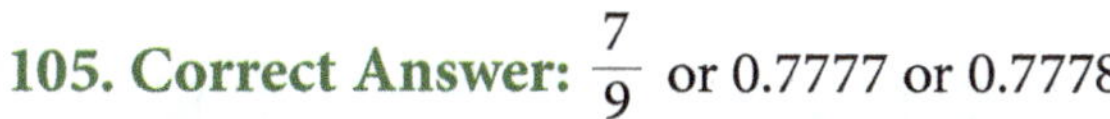

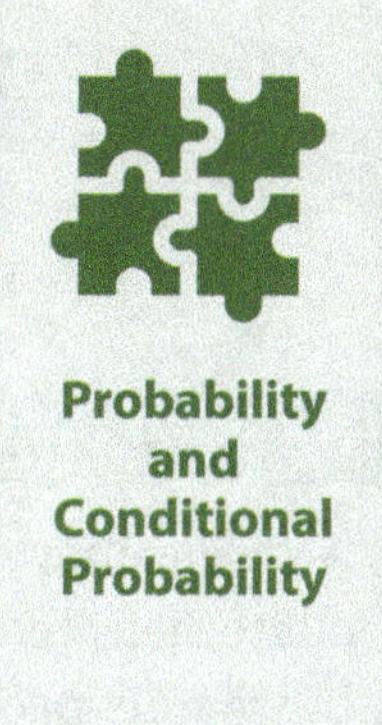

105. Correct Answer: $\frac{7}{9}$ or 0.7777 or 0.7778

This question is a **conditional probability** problem, which means the focus should only be on the relevant rows of the table.

First, identify the total number of books that meet the condition (the denominator). Since we are only looking at books that are not Reference, we only consider the Fiction and Nonfiction rows:

- Total Fiction books: $24 + 18 + 8 = 50$
- Total Nonfiction books: $6 + 22 + 12 = 40$
- Total non-reference books: $50 + 40 = 90$

Next, within this specific group of 90 books, find the number of books that have at most 350 pages. "At most 350" means we include books in both the "200" and "200-350" columns:

- Fiction books with at most 350 pages: $24 + 18 = 42$
- Nonfiction books with at most 350 pages: $6 + 22 = 28$
- Total books meeting both criteria: $42 + 28 = 70$

Finally, create the **probability ratio** using the calculated values:

$$\text{Probability} = \frac{\textit{Number of target books}}{\textit{Total number of non-reference books}}$$

$$\text{Probability} = \frac{70}{90} = \frac{7}{9}$$

Things to Remember:

- "At most" means that the value is the maximum allowed (less than or equal to), while "at least" means the value is the minimum (greater than or equal to).
- Always double-check which rows and columns you are summing to ensure you don't accidentally include data from a category excluded by the prompt.

106 INFERENCE: STATISTICS/ERROR

A researcher surveyed a random sample of 160 customers to estimate the percentage who would buy a new product. The estimate was 62% with a margin of error of $\pm 5\%$ at the same confidence level used throughout. The researcher repeats the study with a random sample of 320 customers and calculates results the same way. Which of the following is the most likely effect of using the larger random sample compared to the smaller one?

A. The margin of error will be lower.

B. The margin of error will be higher.

C. The estimate of the percentage will definitely be lower.

D. The estimate of the percentage will definitely be higher.

107 INFERENCE: STATISTICS/ERROR

A logistics manager took two random samples of package delivery times, in minutes, to estimate the average delivery time from a certain facility. For the first sample, the estimated mean was 42.6 with a margin of error of 2.1. For the second sample, the estimated mean was 43.0 with a margin of error of 3.4. The margins of error were computed the same way at the same confidence level. Which option best explains why the first sample obtained a smaller margin of error than the second sample?

A. The first sample included fewer deliveries than the second sample.

B. The first sample included more deliveries than the second sample.

C. The first sample had a shorter average delivery time than the second sample.

D. The first sample had a longer average delivery time than the second sample.

108 INFERENCE: STATISTICS/ERROR

Sample	Percent saying “improved	Margin of error
M	74.2%	7.1%
N	76.8%	4.2%

Two random samples of employees were asked whether they felt the new training program improved their job performance. The samples were taken from the same company, and the margins of error were calculated using the same method at the same confidence level. Which of the following is the most appropriate reason why the margin of error for Sample M is greater than the margin of error for Sample N?

A. Sample M had a larger sample size.

B. Sample M had a smaller sample size.

C. Sample M had a lower percentage in favor.

D. Sample M had fewer responses recorded as valid.

109 INFERENCE: STATISTICS/ERROR

A polling company selected two random samples of voters in a city to estimate the percentage who support a new public transportation system. In the first sample, the estimate was that 59% of voters support the system, with a margin of error of 8.4%. In the second sample, the estimate was that 62% of voters support the system, with a margin of error of 5.1%. Both margins of error were calculated at the same confidence level using the same method. Which of the following best explains why the second sample obtained a smaller margin of error than the first sample?

A. The first sample had a lower percentage of voters in favor.

B. The first sample had a higher percentage of voters in favor.

C. The first sample contained fewer voters than the second sample.

D. The first sample contained more voters than the second sample.

110 INFERENCE: STATISTICS/ERROR

Total students surveyed	Reported attending groups	Did not report attending study groups
1000	620	380

In a survey of 1,000 randomly selected college students, 62% reported that they regularly attend study groups. The margin of error for this estimate is 4%, calculated at the same confidence level used throughout. Which of the following is a correct statement based on the given margin of error?

A. Exactly 62% of all college students regularly attend study groups.

B. The true percentage of all college students who regularly attend study groups is exactly 66%.

C. About 4% of the students in the study were misclassified as attending study groups.

D. It is unlikely that the true percentage of all college students who regularly attend study groups is greater than 66%.

SEE SOLUTIONS ON NEXT PAGE

ANSWER KEY

QUESTIONS 106-110	
106	A
107	B
108	B
109	C
110	D

106. Correct Answer: A. The margin of error will be lower.

In statistics, the **margin of error** is inversely related to the **sample size.** This means that as the sample size increases, the margin of error decreases.

Because the sample size increased from 160 to 320, the researcher is collecting more data, which leads to a more precise estimate. Consequently, the **margin of error** for the larger sample will be lower than that of the smaller sample.

Things to Remember:

- A larger random sample size generally results in a smaller margin of error and a more reliable estimate of the population parameter.
- As sample size (n) increases, the margin of error decreases.

107. Correct Answer: B. The first sample included more deliveries than the second sample.

The margin of error (MOE) is a measure of the precision of a sample statistic. There are two primary ways to change the margin of error:

- Change the **confidence level** (higher confidence requires a larger **MOE**).
- Change the **sample size** (larger samples result in a smaller **MOE**).

The problem states that the **margins of error** were computed the same way at the same confidence level. Therefore, the difference in the **margin of error** must be due to the size of the samples.

Since Sample 1 has a smaller margin of error, it represents a more precise estimate. For Sample 1 to be more precise than Sample 2 at the same confidence level, it must have utilized a larger number of observations. Thus, the first sample likely included more deliveries than the second sample.

Things to Remember:

- If the confidence level is constant, the only way to obtain a smaller margin of error is to increase the sample size.
- The value of the estimated mean (the average) is independent of the margin of error's size.
- Smaller margins of error indicate that the sample mean is likely closer to the true population mean.

108. Correct Answer: B. Sample M had a smaller sample size.

In statistical studies, the **margin of error** represents the range within which the true population value is likely to fall. The size of this margin is primarily influenced by two factors: **the confidence level** and the **sample size.** The problem states that both **margins of error** were calculated using the same method at the same confidence level.

When the confidence level is held constant, there is an inverse relationship between sample size and the margin of error.

According to the table, Sample M has a margin of error of 7.1%, while Sample N has a smaller margin of error of 4.2%. Since Sample M's margin of error is greater, it is most likely because Sample M had a smaller sample size than Sample N.

Things to Remember:

- A larger sample size leads to a smaller margin of error, assuming all other factors remain the same.

109. Correct Answer: C. The first sample contained fewer voters than the second sample.

The **margin of error (MOE)** measures the reliability of a survey's results. According to the data provided:

Both **margins of error** were calculated at the same **confidence level** using the same method. This means the difference in **MOE** must be attributed to the size of the samples. A larger **sample size** provides more data points, which reduces the uncertainty of the estimate and results in a lower **margin of error.**

Since the second sample has a lower margin of error (5.1%) than the first sample (8.4%), the second sample must have had a larger number of voters. Conversely, the first sample must have contained fewer voters than the second sample.

Things to Remember:

- A decrease in the margin of error is a direct indicator that the sample size was increased.

110. Correct Answer: D. It is unlikely that the true percentage of all college students who regularly attend study groups is greater than 66%.

A **margin of error** provides a range of values, or an "interval," where the true population parameter is likely to be found. To find this interval, you add and subtract the margin of error from the sample estimate:

- Lower bound of the interval: 62% – 4% = 58%
- Upper bound of the interval: 62% + 4% = 66%

This means that based on the survey, the true percentage of all college students who regularly attend study groups is likely between 58% and 66%. Therefore, it is unlikely that the true percentage is greater than 66%.

Things to Remember:

- A margin of error creates a likely range for the true population value (Estimate ± Margin of Error).

111 EVALUATING STATISTICAL CLAIMS

A school district conducted a study on how much time students in grades 9, 10, and 11 spent on homework each week. A total of 120 students were selected at random from one high school in the district. Each student reported the number of hours spent on homework per week, and the data were used to estimate the average number of homework hours for all students in grades 9–11 in the U.S. Which of the following aspects of the study prevents the results from being generalized to all students in grades 9–11 in the U.S.?

A. The selected students were not all from the same grade.

B. The number of selected students was relatively small.

C. The students were selected from only one school in one district.

D. The number of hours reported by each student could have been inaccurate.

SEE SOLUTIONS ON NEXT PAGE

ANSWER KEY

QUESTIONS 111	
111	C

111. Correct Answer: C. The students were selected from only one school in one district.

The question asks to identify the specific aspect of the study that prevents the results from being generalized to all students in grades 9–11 in the United States. Generalizing results from a sample to a larger population requires that the sample be representative of that entire population. In this study:

- The target population is all students in grades 9–11 in the entire U.S.
- The actual sample was taken from only one high school in one district.

Because the students were selected from such a limited geographical area, their homework habits may be influenced by specific local factors, such as district-wide policies, school culture, or regional socioeconomics. These students are not representative of the diverse population of students across the thousands of other districts in the U.S. Therefore, the results cannot be reliably applied to the national level.

Things to Remember:

- To generalize findings to a broad population, the sample must be randomly selected from that specific broad population.
- You can only generalize results to the population from which the random sample was drawn.

GEOMETRY AND TRIGONOMETRY

112 AREA AND VOLUME

A right rectangular prism has a base area of $35t$ square centimeters. The length of the base is 12 cm, and the height of the prism is 7 cm. Which expression represents the surface area, in cm^2, of the prism?

A. $420t + 168$

B. $70t + 336$

C. $\frac{665t}{6} + 168$

D. $\frac{665t}{6} + 84$

113 AREA AND VOLUME

Two similar triangles have corresponding side lengths in the ratio 1:5. The area of the smaller triangle is 28 square units. What is the area, in square units, of the larger triangle?

A. 140

B. 560

C. 700

D. 2800

114 AREA AND VOLUME

Trapezoid ABCD is similar to trapezoid EFGH. The area of ABCD is 12 square centimeters, and the area of EFGH is 108 square centimeters. By what factor is each side length of trapezoid EFGH longer than the corresponding side length of trapezoid ABCD?

A. 3

B. 6

C. 9

D. 12

115 AREA AND VOLUME

Two right square pyramids have congruent square bases each with an area of 144 cm^2. The first pyramid has height 12 cm and the second has height 24 cm. Which of the following is closest to the difference, in cm^2, between their total surface areas?

A. 188

B. 272

C. 316

D. 349

GEOMETRY AND TRIGONOMETRY

116 AREA AND VOLUME

Rectangle WXYZ is similar to rectangle RSTU. The area of rectangle WXYZ is 500 square inches, and the area of rectangle RSTU is 80 square inches. The length of the longest side of rectangle WXYZ is 35 inches. What is the length, in inches, of the longest side of rectangle RSTU?

A. 10

B. 12

C. 14

D. 20

117 AREA AND VOLUME

A rectangular poster has an area of 3,200 square inches. A copy of the poster is made in which the length is increased by 20 percent and the width is increased by 20 percent. What is the area of the copy, in square inches?

A. 3,840

B. 4,164

C. 4,545

D. 4,608

118 AREA AND VOLUME

A rectangular region is partitioned into 45 square lots of equal area R square units. The length of the region is 1.25 times its width. If the width of the region is xR units, what is the value of x?

119 AREA AND VOLUME

Two similar right triangles PQR and STU have corresponding sides in the ratio STU:PQR = 3.5:1. The area of triangle PQR is 48 square units. What is the area, in square units, of triangle STU?

A. 168

B. 336

C. 588

D. 1,176

120 AREA AND VOLUME

A right circular cone has a total surface area of 384π square centimeters, and the lateral surface area of the cone is 240π square centimeters. What is the height, in centimeters, of the cone?

A. 12

B. 16

C. 20

D. 28

SEE SOLUTIONS ON NEXT PAGE

ANSWER KEY

QUESTIONS 112-120	
112	C
113	C
114	A
115	B
116	C
117	D
118	6
119	C
120	B

112. Correct Answer: C. $\frac{665t}{6} + 168$

To find the **surface area** of a **right rectangular prism**, we need the dimensions of the base (length and width) and the height of the prism.

First, find the width (w) of the base using the base area formula:

$$\text{base area} = \text{length} \times \text{width}$$

$$35t = 12w$$

$$\frac{35t}{12} = w$$

Next, find the perimeter of the base:

$$\text{perimeter} = 2(\text{length} + \text{width})$$

$$p = 2(12 + \frac{35t}{12})$$

$$p = 24 + \frac{35t}{6}$$

Now, use the surface area formula for a prism to calculate the equation:

$SA = 2(\text{Base Area}) + (\text{Perimeter} \times \text{Height})$

$SA = 2(35t) + ((24 + \frac{35t}{6}) \times 7)$ Plug-in known values

$SA = 70t + 168 + \frac{245t}{6}$ Distribute

$SA = \frac{665t}{6} + 168$ Simplify

Things to Remember:

- The surface area of a prism is the sum of the areas of all its faces.
- The lateral area of a right prism can be calculated as the perimeter of the base multiplied by the height.

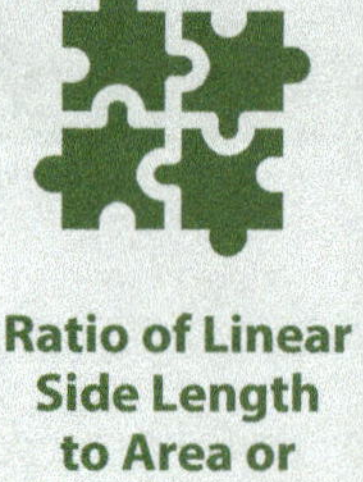

Ratio of Linear Side Length to Area or Volume

113. Correct Answer: C. 700

For similar figures, the ratio of areas is the square of the ratio of corresponding side lengths. If the ratio of side lengths is $a:b$, then the ratio of their areas is $a^2:b^2$.

$$\text{Given side length ratio} = 1:5$$

$$\text{Area ratio} = 1^2:5^2 = 1:25$$

This means the larger triangle is 25 times the area of the smaller triangle.

$$\text{Area of larger triangle} = 28 \times 25$$

$$\text{Area of larger triangle} = 700$$

Things to Remember:

- Always ensure you are squaring the linear scale factor when moving from length to area.

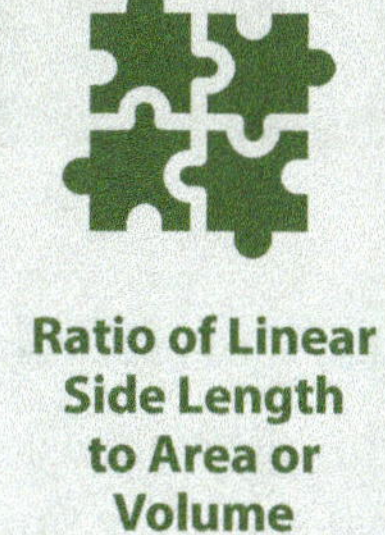

Ratio of Linear Side Length to Area or Volume

114. Correct Answer: A. 3

For **similar figures**, the ratio of the areas is equal to the square of the ratio of their corresponding side lengths. For trapezoid ABCD and trapezoid EFGH, the area ratio is:

$$\frac{\text{area trapezoid ABCD}}{\text{area trapezoid EFGH}} = \frac{108}{12} = 9$$

Use the area ratio to find the ratio of their corresponding side lengths:

$9 = k^2$

$3 = k$ Square root

Therefore, each side length of trapezoid EFGH is 3 times longer than the corresponding side length of trapezoid ABCD.

Things to Remember:

- To find the side length ratio when given the area ratio, take the square root of the area ratio.
- "Similar" figures have proportional side lengths and identical corresponding angles.

SOLUTIONS
AREA AND VOLUME

Surface Area

115. Correct Answer: B. 272

This problem asks to find the difference in total **surface area** between two right square pyramids that share the same base area but have different heights. To find the surface area of a pyramid, the base area and lateral area are needed. The base area is given, but it can be used to find the side lengths which will be needed for the lateral area:

Start by finding the base dimensions by taking the square root of the area:

$$\text{side length} = \sqrt{144} = 15$$

Evaluate the equation for total surface area of a pyramid to determine what needs to be solved for next:

$$\text{Total Surface Area} = \text{Base Area} + \text{Lateral Area}$$

$$\text{Lateral Area} = 2 \times \text{base} \times \text{slant height}$$

Since both pyramids have the same Base Area, the difference in total surface area is simply the difference in their Lateral Areas. The slant height is needed to calculate the lateral area so next calculate Slant Height (L) for each pyramid using the Pythagorean theorem:

$$L = \sqrt{h^2 + (\tfrac{s}{2})^2}$$

For Pyramid 1 ($h = 12, s = 12$):

$$L = \sqrt{12^2 + (\tfrac{12}{2})^2} = \sqrt{144 + 36} = \sqrt{180} \approx 13.416$$

For Pyramid 2 ($h = 24, s = 12$):

$$L = \sqrt{24^2 + (\tfrac{12}{2})^2} = \sqrt{576 + 36} = \sqrt{612} \approx 24.738$$

Now, use these slant heights to calculate the lateral area of each pyramid:

Lateral Area 1:

$$2 \times 12 \times \sqrt{180} = 24 \times 13.416 \approx 321.98$$

Lateral Area 2:

$$\times 12 \times \sqrt{612} = 24 \times 24.738 \approx 593.71$$

Finally, find the difference between the two lateral areas to determine the difference in surface area:

$$593.71 - 321.98 = 271.73$$

Rounding to the nearest whole number, the difference is 272.

Things to Remember:

- The slant height of a pyramid is the altitude of a triangular lateral face, not the vertical height of the pyramid.
- Use the Pythagorean theorem with the height and half the base side length to find the slant height.
- Surface area is the sum of the base area and the lateral area (the area of the four triangular faces).

Ratio of Linear Side Length to Area or Volume

116. Correct Answer: C. 14

To determine the length of the longest side of rectangle RSTU, first determine the ratio of the **areas** of the two **similar** rectangles:

$$\frac{\text{Area of WXYZ}}{\text{Area of RSTU}} = \frac{500}{80} = 6.25$$

Because the rectangles are similar, the ratio of their areas is equal to the square of the ratio of their corresponding side lengths, often referred to as the **scale factor** (k):

$$k^2 = 6.25$$

$$k = \sqrt{6.25} = 2.5$$

This means every side in rectangle WXYZ is 2.5 times longer than the corresponding side in rectangle RSTU. Since the longest side of WXYZ is 35 inches, divide by the scale factor to find the longest side of RSTU:

$$\text{Longest side of RSTU} = \frac{35}{2.5} = 14$$

Things to Remember:

- For similar figures, the ratio of areas is the square of the ratio of corresponding side lengths.
- To find a missing side length when areas are known, first find the linear scale factor by taking the square root of the area ratio.

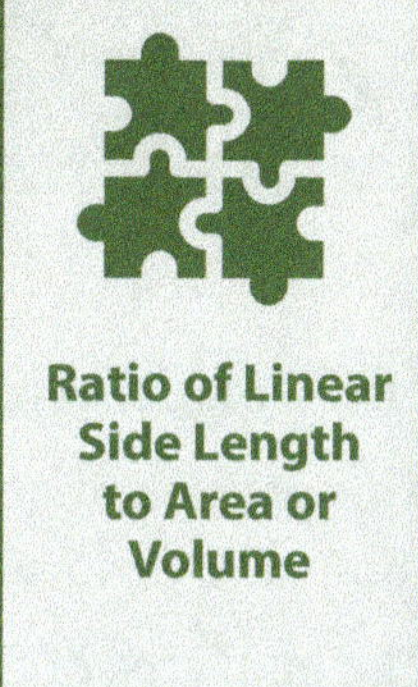

117. Correct Answer: D. 4,608

Identify the **scale factor** for the side lengths. An increase of 20% is equivalent to multiplying the original dimension by 1.20:

$$\text{increase of } 20\% \rightarrow 120\% \rightarrow \times\ 1.20$$

The area of a rectangle scales based on the product of the length and width scale factors. Since both dimensions increase by the same factor, the area scales by the square of that factor:

$$\text{Area scale factor} = 1.20 \times 1.20 = 1.44$$

Multiply the original area of the poster by the area scale factor of 1.44 to determine the new area:

$$\text{New Area} = 3{,}200 \times 1.44 = 4{,}608$$

Things to Remember:

- A percentage increase can be represented as a decimal multiplier.
- If all linear dimensions of a figure are multiplied by a factor k, the area is multiplied by $k2$.

118. Correct Answer: 6

This problem requires setting up an algebraic equation for the area of a large rectangular region composed of 45 smaller square lots, each with area R.

The total area of the region is the sum of the areas of the 45 lots:

$$\text{Total Area} = 45\text{R}$$

The problem provides dimensions for the region in terms of x and the square root of R:

$$\text{Width} = x\sqrt{\text{R}}$$

$$\text{Length} = 1.25 \times \text{width} = 1.25\ x\sqrt{\text{R}}$$

Set up the area formula for the rectangle and set it equal to the total area:

$$\text{Area} = \text{length} \times \text{width}$$

$$45\text{R} = 1.25x\ \sqrt{\text{R}} \times x\sqrt{\text{R}}$$

Simplify to evaluate x:

$45\text{R} = 1.25\,x\sqrt{\text{R}} \times x\sqrt{\text{R}}$	
$45\text{R} = 1.25x^2\ \text{R}$	Multiply
$45 = 1.25x^2$	Cancel R
$36 = x^2$	Divide
$x = 6$	Square root

Things to Remember:

- Relate the total area of a subdivided region to the area of its individual components to solve for unknowns.

SOLUTIONS
AREA AND VOLUME

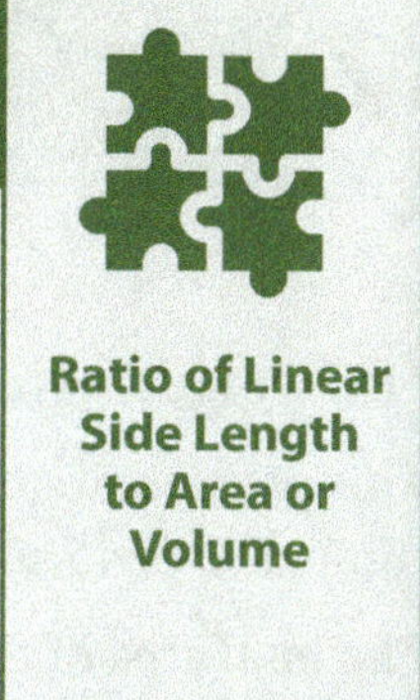

117. Correct Answer: D. 4,608

Identify the **scale factor** for the side lengths. An increase of 20% is equivalent to multiplying the original dimension by 1.20:

increase of 20% → 120% → × 1.20

The area of a rectangle scales based on the product of the length and width scale factors. Since both dimensions increase by the same factor, the area scales by the square of that factor:

Area scale factor = 1.20 × 1.20 = 1.44

Multiply the original area of the poster by the area scale factor of 1.44 to determine the new area:

New Area = 3,200 × 1.44 = 4,608

Things to Remember:

- A percentage increase can be represented as a decimal multiplier.
- If all linear dimensions of a figure are multiplied by a factor k, the area is multiplied by *k*2.

118. Correct Answer: 6

This problem requires setting up an algebraic equation for the area of a large rectangular region composed of 45 smaller square lots, each with area R.

The total area of the region is the sum of the areas of the 45 lots:

$$\text{Total Area} = 45R$$

The problem provides dimensions for the region in terms of x and the square root of R:

$$\text{Width} = x\sqrt{R}$$

$$\text{Length} = 1.25 \times \text{width} = 1.25\ x\sqrt{R}$$

Set up the area formula for the rectangle and set it equal to the total area:

$$\text{Area} = \text{length} \times \text{width}$$

$$45R = 1.25x\ \sqrt{R} \times x\sqrt{R}$$

Simplify to evaluate x:

$45R = 1.25\,x\sqrt{R} \times x\sqrt{R}$

$45R = 1.25x^2\,R$	Multiply
$45 = 1.25x^2$	Cancel R
$36 = x^2$	Divide
$x = 6$	Square root

Things to Remember:

- Relate the total area of a subdivided region to the area of its individual components to solve for unknowns.

119. Correct Answer: C. 588

The ratio of the sides is given as STU:PQR = 3.5 :1. This means triangle STU has side lengths 3.5 times longer than those of PQR.

To find the area ratio, square the ratio of the side lengths:

$$(3.5 : 1)^2 = 12.25 : 1$$

This means the area of triangle STU is 12.25 times the area of triangle PQR. Multiply the given area of PQR (48 square units) by this factor:

$$48 \times 12.25 = 588$$

Things to Remember:

- The ratio of the areas of similar triangles is the square of the ratio of their corresponding side lengths.

120. Correct Answer: B. 16

To solve for the vertical height of a right circular cone use the surface area equation:

Total surface area = Base area + Lateral surface area

The total surface area and the lateral surface area are given. Use them to calculate the base area:

$$\text{Total surface area} = \text{Base area} + \text{Lateral surface area}$$

$$384\pi = x + 240\pi$$

$$x = 144\pi$$

To find the vertical height, the radius and the slant height need to be found first. To find the radius (r) of the base, use the base area:

$$\text{Base area} = \pi r^2$$

$$144\pi = \pi r^2$$

$$144 = r^2$$

$$r = 12$$

Next, find the slant height (l) using the lateral area:

$$\text{Lateral area} = \pi r l$$

$$240\pi = \pi 12 l$$

$$240 = 12l$$

$$l = 20$$

Solve for the vertical height (h) using the Pythagorean theorem, as the radius, height, and slant height form a right triangle:

$$r^2 + h^2 = l^2$$

$$12^2 + h^2 = 20^2$$

$$144 + h^2 = 400$$

$$h^2 = 256$$

$$h = 16$$

Things to Remember:

- The total surface area of a right circular cone is equal to the sum of its base area and lateral surface area.
- Use the Pythagorean theorem to find the vertical height when the radius and slant height are known.

GEOMETRY AND TRIGONOMETRY

121 LINES, ANGLES, AND TRIANGLES

A line intersects two parallel lines, creating four acute angles and four obtuse angles. One obtuse angle measures $(8x + 50)°$. The sum of three of the acute angles and one of the obtuse angles is $(-16x + t)°$. What is the value of t?

122 LINES, ANGLES, AND TRIANGLES

A line intersects two parallel lines, forming four acute angles and four obtuse angles. The measure of one acute angle is $(6x - 220)°$. Let k be the sum of the measures of four of the eight angles. Which of the following could NOT be equal to k?

A. 360

B. $-24x + 1600$

C. $24x - 880$

D. $-12x + 1020$

123 LINES, ANGLES, AND TRIANGLES

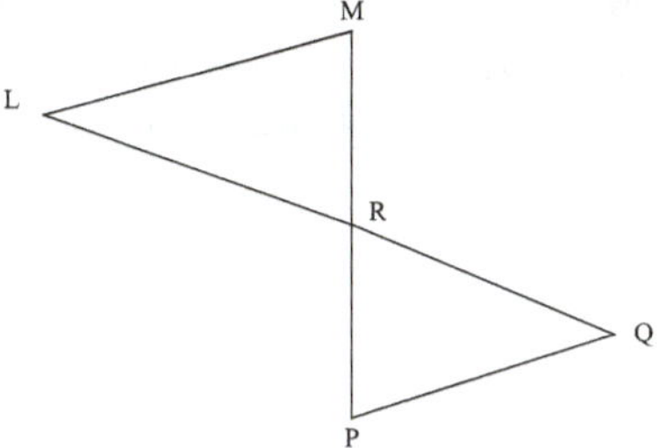

In the figure, LQ intersects MP at point R, and LM is parallel to PQ. The lengths MR, LR, and RP are 13, 15, and 22, respectively. What is the length of LQ?

A. $\frac{330}{13}$

B. $\frac{495}{13}$

C. $\frac{525}{13}$

D. $\frac{580}{13}$

124 LINES, ANGLES, AND TRIANGLES

In triangles ABC and DEF, side BC equals side EF, and angle A equals angle D. Which additional piece of information is sufficient to prove that triangle ABC is congruent to triangle DEF?

A. AC equals DF

B. AB equals DE

C. angle B equals angle E

D. angle C equals angle D

GEOMETRY AND TRIGONOMETRY

125 LINES, ANGLES, AND TRIANGLES

A regular polygon has exactly 73 sides. If the measure of each of the 73 interior angles of this polygon is $180p°$, what is the value of p?

126 LINES, ANGLES, AND TRIANGLES

In isosceles triangle XYZ, sides XY and XZ are congruent. Point A lies on YZ such that YA:YZ = 3:7. Through A, a line parallel to XZ meets XY at B, and a line parallel to XY meets XZ at C. If YB = 15, what is the length of ZC?

A. 20

B. 25

C. 35

D. 40

127 LINES, ANGLES, AND TRIANGLES

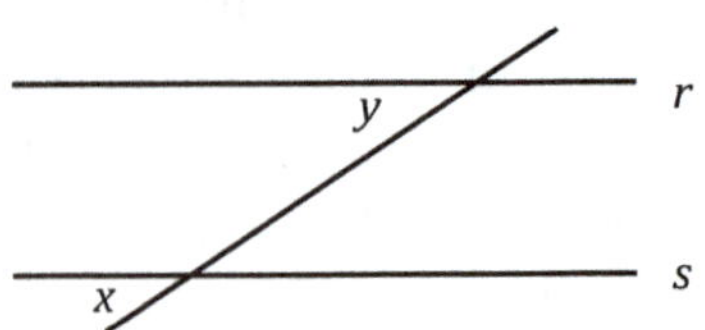

Lines r and s are parallel. Another line t intersects both lines. Angle x at the intersection with line r and angle y at the intersection with line s are alternate interior angles. If $x = 2w + 31$, $y = 5w - 17$, and $a = 9w - 5$, find the value of a.

128 LINES, ANGLES, AND TRIANGLES

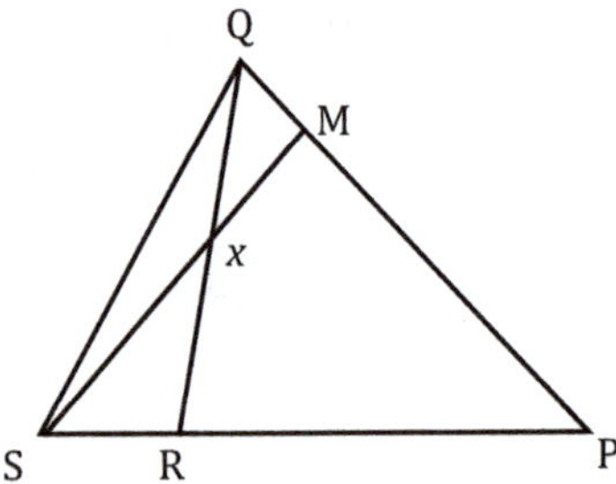

In the figure, point M lies on side PQ of triangle PQR and MS = MP. If $\angle$ QMS = 28° and $\angle$ PRQ = 41°, what is the measure of x?

CONTINUE

129 LINES, ANGLES, AND TRIANGLES

In triangles PQR and XYZ, side PQ equals side XY, each with length 8, and angle P equals angle X, each measuring 50°. Which of the following additional pieces of information is sufficient to determine whether triangle PQR is congruent to triangle XYZ?

I. Angles Q and Y are equal.

II. Sides PR and XZ are equal.

III. Sides PQ and YZ are equal.

A. I only

B. II only

C. III only

D. I and II

ANSWER KEY

QUESTIONS 121-129	
121	440
122	D
123	C
124	C
125	71/73
126	A
127	139
128	153
129	D

121. Correct Answer: 440

When a line intersects two parallel lines, it creates eight angles: four equal **acute** angles and four equal **obtuse** angles. Any one **acute** angle and any one **obtuse** angle are **supplementary**, meaning their sum is 180 degrees.

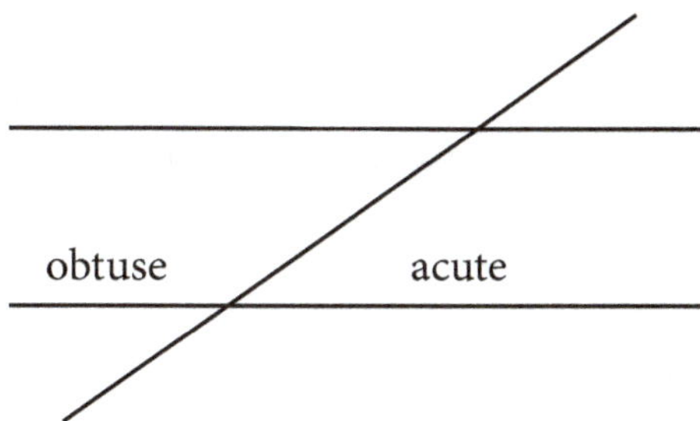

The problem states that an obtuse angle measures $(8x + 50)$ degrees. To find the measure of an acute angle, subtract the obtuse angle from 180:

$$\text{acute angle} = 180 - (8x + 50)$$

$$\text{acute angle} = 130 - 8x$$

Next, create an equation based on the sum provided in the problem. The sum of three acute angles and one obtuse angle is given as $(-16x + t)$ degrees:

$$3 \text{ acute} + 1 \text{ obtuse} = 16x + t$$

$$3(130 - 8x) + (8x + 50) = -16x + t$$

Use this equation to solve for t:

$3(130 - 8x) + (8x + 50) = -16x + t$	
$390 - 24x + 8x + 50 = -16x + t$	Distribute
$440 - 16x = -16x + t$	Simplify
$440 = t$	Cancel out x

Things to Remember:

- In a parallel line and transversal intersection, any acute angle and any obtuse angle are supplementary (sum to 180 degrees).

SOLUTIONS

LINES, ANGLES, AND TRIANGLES

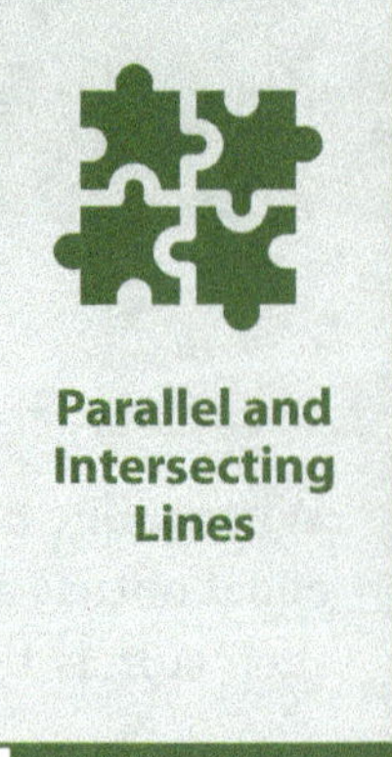

122. Correct Answer: D. -12x + 1020

In this scenario, there are four **acute** angles and four **obtuse** angles. An **acute** angle and an **obtuse** angle on the same line must sum to 180 degrees. Since the acute angle measures $(6x - 220)$ degrees the obtuse angle can be found through subtraction:

$$180 - (6x - 220) = 400 - 6x$$

The value k is the sum of any four of these eight angles. Let m be the number of acute angles used (where m is an integer from 0 to 4). The number of obtuse angles used would then be $(4 - m)$. Use this relationship to create an equation for k:

$$k = m(6x - 220) + (4 - m)(400 - 6x)$$

$$k = 6mx - 220m + 1600 - 24x - 400m + 6mx$$

$$k = 12mx - 620m - 24x + 1600$$

Evaluate k for each possible value of m:

- $m = 0$ (4 obtuse): $k = 1600 - 24x$ (Choice B)
- $m = 1$ (1 acute, 3 obtuse): $k = -12x + 980$
- $m = 2$ (2 acute, 2 obtuse): $k = 360$ (Choice A)
- $m = 3$ (3 acute, 1 obtuse): $k = 12x - 260$
- $m = 4$ (4 acute): $k = 24x - 880$ (Choice C)

Comparing these results to the options, Choice D $(-12x + 1020)$ is not a possible sum for k.

Things to Remember:

- An acute and obtuse angle that lie on the same line must add to 180 degrees.

123. Correct Answer: C. $\frac{525}{13}$

Start by determining the relationship between the two triangles. Because LM is parallel to PQ, the alternate interior angles are equal (angle L = angle Q and angle M = angle P). Additionally, the angles at point R are vertical angles and are therefore equal. This means triangle LRM and triangle QRP are similar.

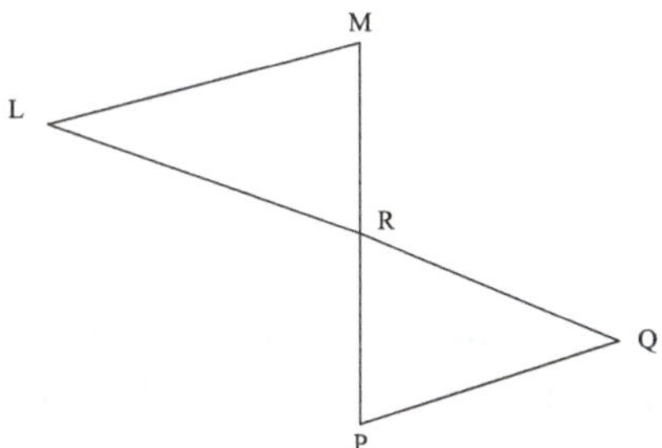

Since the triangles are similar, their corresponding side lengths are proportional. Use the given side lengths within the proportion to determine the value of RQ:

$\frac{LR}{RQ} = \frac{MR}{RP}$

$\frac{15}{RQ} = \frac{13}{22}$ Substitute

$13RQ = 15(22)$ Cross-multiply

$13RQ = 330$ Simplify

$RQ = \frac{330}{13}$ Divide

The question asks for the length of segment LQ. Since R is a point on segment LQ, add LR and RQ together to evaluate:

$LQ = LR + RQ$

$LQ = 15 + \frac{330}{13}$ Substitute

$LQ = \frac{525}{13}$ Simplify

Things to Remember:

- Parallel lines with transversals often create similar triangles through equal alternate interior angles.
- In similar triangles, set up a proportion comparing corresponding sides.
- Always ensure you are solving for the final value requested rather than just a portion of it.

124. Correct Answer: C. angle B equals angle E

It is given that side BC equals side EF and angle A equals angle D. To prove the triangles are congruent, one of the **congruence postulates** such as SAS, ASA, or AAS must be use.

From the problem it is confirmed that:

- Side BC corresponds to side EF.
- Angle A corresponds to angle D.

This provides one Side (S) and one Angle (A). To use the AAS (Angle-Angle-Side) theorem, we need a second pair of corresponding angles. Therefore, Choice C can be used to establish that angle B equals angle E, which is sufficient to prove congruence via the AAS postulate.

Things to Remember:

- Congruence postulates include SSS, SAS, ASA, AAS, and HL.
- Congruency requires both side lengths and angles to be congruent. Similarity just requires angles to be congruent.

125. Correct Answer: $\frac{71}{73}$

To find the measure of an interior angle of a regular polygon, you must first calculate the sum of all interior angles. The formula for the sum of the interior angles of a polygon with n sides is $S = 180(n - 2)$.

For a regular polygon with exactly 73 sides ($n = 73$):

$S = 180(73 - 2)$	Plug-in
$S = 180(71)$	Subtract
$S = 12{,}780$	Multiply

In a regular polygon, every interior angle is identical. To find the measure of a single interior angle, divide the total sum of the angles by the total number of sides:

$$\text{Measure of each angle} = \frac{12{,}780}{73}$$

The problem states that the measure of each of these 73 interior angles is 180p degrees. Set up an equation to solve for p:

$$180p = \frac{12{,}780}{73} \rightarrow p = \frac{71}{73}$$

Things to Remember:

- The sum of the interior angles of a polygon is found with $S = 180(n - 2)$, where n represents the number of sides.
- In a regular polygon, you can find the measure of one interior angle by dividing the total sum of angles by the number of sides.

CONTINUE

126. Correct Answer: A. 20

In isosceles triangle XYZ, the sides XY and XZ are congruent. This equality establishes a set of proportional relationships between the segments of the triangle when parallel lines are introduced.

The problem defines point A on YZ such that the ratio YA:YZ = 3:7. This means YA is 3/7 of the total length of YZ. When a line through A is drawn parallel to XZ meeting XY at B, it creates a smaller triangle YBA that is similar to triangle YXZ. This similarity gives the proportion:

$$\frac{YB}{XY} = \frac{YA}{YZ} = \frac{3}{7}$$

Substitute the given value YB = 15 into the proportion to solve for XY:

$\frac{15}{XY} = \frac{3}{7}$

$7(15) = 3XY$	Cross multiply
$105 = 3XY$	Simplify
$XY = 35$	Divide

Because the triangle is isosceles (XY = XZ), the length of XZ is also 35.

Next, a second line is drawn through A parallel to XY meeting XZ at C. This creates another similar relationship where:

$$\frac{ZC}{XZ} = \frac{ZA}{YZ}$$

Since YA is $\frac{3}{7}$ of YZ, the segment ZA must be $\frac{4}{7}$ of YZ (YA + YZ = ZA). Therefore:

$$\frac{ZC}{XZ} = \frac{4}{7}$$

Using the value XZ = 35, calculate the length of ZC:

$\frac{ZC}{35} = \frac{4}{7}$

$7ZC = 4(35)$	Cross multiply
$7ZC = 140$	Simplify
$ZC = 20$	Divide

Things to Remember:

- In an isosceles triangle, two sides are equal in length.
- Lines drawn parallel to one side of a triangle create smaller, similar triangles whose sides are proportional to the original triangle.

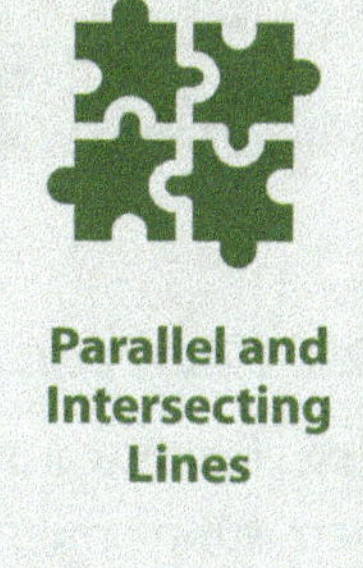

127. Correct Answer: 139

Lines r and s are **parallel**, and they are intersected by a **transversal** line t. In this geometric configuration, **alternate interior angles** are equal. The problem identifies angles x and y as alternate interior angles, so $x = y$.

Set the expressions for x and y equal to each other to solve for w:

$x = y \rightarrow 2w + 31 = 5w - 17$

$31 + 17 = 5w - 2w$	Combine like terms
$48 = 3w$	Simplify
$w = 16$	Divide

The question asks for the value of a, which is defined by the expression $a = 9w - 5$. Substitute the value $w = 16$ into this expression to solve for a:

$a = 9(16) - 5$	Substitute
$a = 144 - 5$	Multiply
$a = 139$	Subtract

Things to Remember:

- When a transversal intersects parallel lines, alternate interior angles are always congruent.

128. Correct Answer: 153

First, find the angles related to point M. Angle QMS and angle SMP lie on a straight line, making them supplementary:

$$\text{Angle SMP} = 180 - \text{Angle QMS}$$

$$\text{Angle SMP} = 180 - 28 = 152$$

In triangle SMP, we are given that MS = MP, making it an isosceles triangle. In an isosceles triangle, the angles opposite the equal sides are also equal (Angle MSP = Angle MPS). The sum of angles in triangle SMP is 180 degrees:

$$152 + 2x = 180$$

$$2x = 28$$

$$x = 14$$

Thus, Angle MPS (which is angle P) is 14 degrees and Angle MSP (angle S) is 14 degrees.

To find the value of x, consider the sum of the interior angles of a quadrilateral, which is 360 degrees. For the quadrilateral formed in this figure:

$$x + \text{Angle R} + \text{Angle SMP} + \text{Angle P} = 360$$

Substitute the known values to solve:

$$x + 41 + 152 + 14 = 360$$

$$x + 207 = 360$$

$$x = 153$$

Things to Remember:

- The sum of angles on a straight line is 180 degrees.
- In an isosceles triangle, the base angles (the angles opposite the equal sides) are equal.
- The interior angles of any quadrilateral always sum to 360 degrees.

129. Correct Answer: D. I and II

The question provides that side PQ = XY = 8 and angle P = Angle X = 50 degrees. This establishes one side (S) and one angle (A) that are congruent between triangles PQR and XYZ. To determine if the triangles are congruent, we need a third piece of information that satisfies a congruence postulate.

- **Option I: Angles Q and Y are equal.** This would give two angles and the included side (ASA) or two angles and a non-included side (AAS). This is sufficient to prove congruence.
- **Option II: Sides PR and XZ are equal.** This would give two sides and the included angle (SAS). This is sufficient to prove congruence.
- **Option III: Sides PQ and YZ are equal.** This relates sides that do not necessarily establish a standard congruence pattern given the current known values.

Therefore, both Options I and II provide enough additional information to prove congruence.

Things to Remember:

- Common triangle congruence postulates include SSS, SAS, ASA, and AAS.
- When checking for congruency, identify which parts (sides or angles) are corresponding and how they are positioned relative to each other.

GEOMETRY AND TRIGONOMETRY

130 RIGHT TRIANGLES AND TRIGONOMETRY

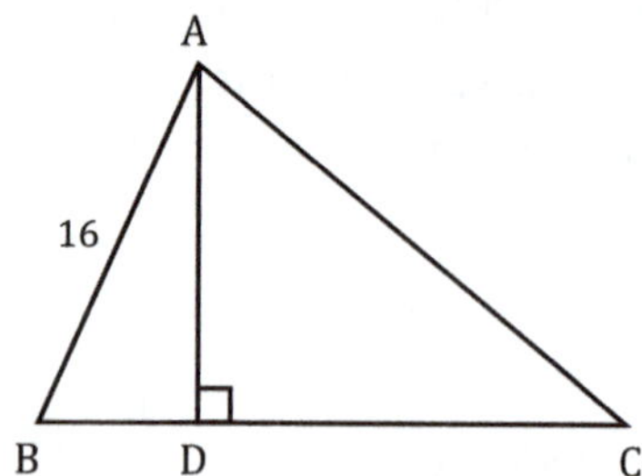

In the figure shown, the measure of angle A is 40°, side AB is 16 units, and side AC is 26 units. What is the area of triangle ABC?

A. 208

B. 416

C. 208sin(40°)

D. 416sin(40°)

131 RIGHT TRIANGLES AND TRIGONOMETRY

The perimeter of an isosceles right triangle is $26 + 26\sqrt{2}$ inches. What is the length, in inches, of the hypotenuse of this triangle?

A. 13

B. $13\sqrt{2}$

C. 26

D. $26\sqrt{2}$

132 RIGHT TRIANGLES AND TRIGONOMETRY

In the xy–plane, the line segment with endpoints (–3, 2) and (5, 11) represents one leg of a right triangle. The area of the triangle is $56\sqrt{145}$ square units. What is the length, in units, of the other leg?

A. 56

B. 80

C. 112

D. $8\sqrt{145}$

133 RIGHT TRIANGLES AND TRIGONOMETRY

In right triangle ABC with right angle at B, the hypotenuse AC has length 15. The length of AB is 10 less than the length of AC. Point D lies on AC such that BD is perpendicular to AC. What is the value of $\frac{BC}{BD}$?

GEOMETRY AND TRIGONOMETRY

134 RIGHT TRIANGLES AND TRIGONOMETRY

What is the value of $\sin\frac{73\pi}{6}$?

A. 0

B. $\frac{1}{2}$

C. $\frac{\sqrt{3}}{2}$

D. $-\frac{1}{2}$

135 RIGHT TRIANGLES AND TRIGONOMETRY

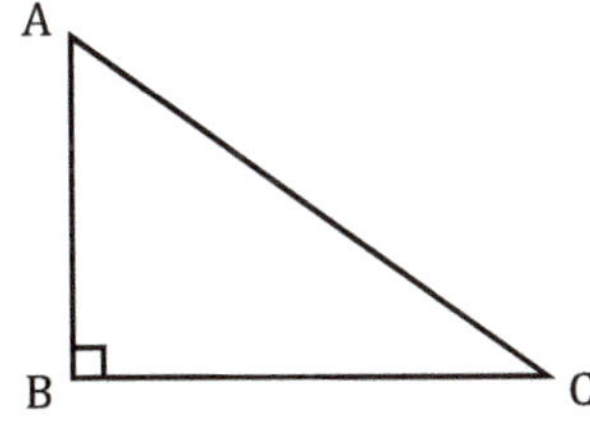

In triangle ABC, ∠B is a right angle and AB < BC. The side BC has length 20. Let θ be the measure of ∠C. Which expression represents the length of AC in terms of θ?

A. $20\cos\theta$

B. $20\sin\theta$

C. $\frac{20}{\sin\theta}$

D. $\frac{20}{\cos\theta}$

136 RIGHT TRIANGLES AND TRIGONOMETRY

In triangle ABC, angle B is a right angle, the measure of angle C is 27°, and the length of BC is 14 units. If the area of triangle ABC can be written in the form $k\tan 27°$, where k is a constant, what is the value of k?

137 RIGHT TRIANGLES AND TRIGONOMETRY

In right triangle JKL, angle J is 90°. If $\sin(K)=\frac{5\sqrt{6}}{13}$, what is the value of $\cos(L)$?

A. $\frac{5\sqrt{6}}{13}$

B. $\frac{5}{13}$

C. $\frac{\sqrt{13}}{6}$

D. $\frac{12}{13}$

CONTINUE

138 RIGHT TRIANGLES AND TRIGONOMETRY

A straight ramp rises to a platform that is 30 inches above level ground. Building rules require the ramp to meet the ground at an angle θ satisfying $\tan\theta \leq 120$. If the horizontal distance from the start of the ramp to the base of the platform is x inches, what is the least possible value of x?

SEE SOLUTIONS ON NEXT PAGE

CONTINUE

ANSWER KEY

QUESTIONS 130-138	
130	C
131	B
132	C
133	3
134	B
135	D
136	98
137	A
138	600

Don't just check the answer—master the method.
Get specific Desmos tips for each solution online. Gain access to The Gauntlet Mock Test and track your progress in real-time at **passthegauntlet.com.** Use code **GAUNTLETMATH20** to unlock 20% off your digital dashboard.

130. Correct Answer: C. 208sin(40°)

The problem asks for the **area** of triangle ABC. While the most common formula for the area of a triangle is Area = $\frac{1}{2}$ base × height, the height is not given so another approach is needed to solve. Instead, use the **trigonometric area formula:**

$$\text{Area} = \frac{1}{2}ab\sin(\theta)$$

$$\text{Area} = \frac{1}{2}(16)(26)\sin(40°) = 208\sin(40°)$$

Note: Alternatively, you could find the height AD by looking at right triangle ABD. Using SOH CAH TOA, sin(40°) = AD / 16, which means the height AD = 16sin(40°). If you plug this into the standard formula using AC (26) as the base, you get: Area = $\frac{1}{2}$ *26 × 16sin(40°), which simplifies to 208sin(40°).*

Things to Remember:

- The area of any triangle can be calculated if you have two sides and the included angle using the formula: Area = $\frac{1}{2}$ absin(θ)

Right Triangle Side Ratios and Theorems

131. Correct Answer: B. $13\sqrt{2}$

An **isosceles right triangle** is a special **45 – 45 – 90 triangle**. These triangles always have a specific ratio for their side lengths: the two legs are equal (x), and the hypotenuse is the leg length times the square root of 2 ($x\sqrt{2}$).

Relate the given perimeter equation to a perimeter expression for 45 – 45 – 90 triangles. The perimeter is the sum of all three sides:

$$\text{Perimeter} = \text{Leg} + \text{Leg} + \text{Hypotenuse}$$

$$26 + 26\sqrt{2} = x + x + x\sqrt{2}$$

$$26 + 26\sqrt{2} = 2x + x\sqrt{2}$$

To evaluate x, the length of the leg of the triangle, match the terms in the expression and simplify. Either expression with result in the same value:

$$26 + 26\sqrt{2} = 2x + x\sqrt{2}$$

$$26 = 2x \rightarrow 13 = x$$

$$26\sqrt{2} = x\sqrt{2} \rightarrow 13 = x$$

The question asks for the length of the hypotenuse ($x\sqrt{2}$):

$$\text{Hypotenuse} = x\sqrt{2} = 13\sqrt{2}$$

Things to Remember:

- The side ratio for a 45 – 45 – 90 triangle is $x : x : x\sqrt{2}$.

132. Correct Answer: C. 112

To find the length of the missing leg, use the area formula and the given leg to solve. To find the length of the leg provided in the coordinate plane use the **distance formula** between the points (-3, 2) and (5, 11):

$$\text{Distance} = \sqrt{(x_2 - x_1)^2 + (y_2 - y_1)^2}$$

$$\text{Distance} = \sqrt{(5 - (-3))^2 + (11 - 2)^2}$$

$$\text{Distance} = \sqrt{(8)^2 + (9)^2} = \sqrt{145}$$

So, the given leg of the right triangle is $\sqrt{145}$ units long. Use the area formula to calculate the length of the other leg:

Area = $\frac{1}{2}$ base × height	
$56\sqrt{145} = \frac{1}{2}(\sqrt{145})x$	Plug-in
$56 = \frac{1}{2}x$	Cancel
$x = 112$	Multiply

Things to Remember:

- The distance formula can be used to calculate the length of the leg of a triangle.

Right Triangle Side Ratios and Theorems

133. Correct Answer: 3

The goal is to find the value of $\frac{BC}{BD}$ in right triangle ABC where B is the right angle, AC = 15, and BD is perpendicular to AC.

First, find the lengths of the legs. The hypotenuse AC has length 15, and AB is 10 less than AC, so AB = 15 − 10 = 5. Use the **Pythagorean theorem** to find BC:

$$AB^2 + BC^2 = AC^2$$

$5^2 + BC^2 = 15^2$ Plug-in

$25 + BC^2 = 225$ Square

$BC^2 = 200$ Subtract

$BC = \sqrt{200}$ Square root

$BC = 10\sqrt{2}$ Simplify

Next, find BD, the altitude from B to the hypotenuse. In a right triangle, the altitude to the hypotenuse can be found using the formula:

$$BD = \frac{AB \times BC}{AC}$$

$BD = \frac{(5 \times 10\sqrt{2})}{15}$ Plug-in

$BD = \frac{(50\sqrt{2})}{15}$ Simplify

$BD = \frac{(10\sqrt{2})}{3}$ Divide

Finally, calculate the ratio:

$$\frac{BC}{BD} = \frac{(10\sqrt{2})}{\frac{(10\sqrt{2})}{3}} = 3$$

Things to Remember:

- The altitude to the hypotenuse creates two smaller triangles that are similar to the original triangle and to each other.

Unit Circle and Trigonometry

134. Correct Answer: B. $\frac{1}{2}$

The problem asks for the value of sin $\frac{73\pi}{6}$. To find this value, simplify the angle by finding a coterminal angle between 0 and 2π.

One full rotation is 2π, so find a multiple of 2π that is closest to $\frac{73\pi}{6}$.

$$2\pi = \frac{12\pi}{6}$$

$$\frac{12\pi}{6} \times 6 = \frac{72\pi}{6}$$

Subtract $\frac{72\pi}{6}$ from $\frac{73\pi}{6}$ to determine the remaining angle left over:

$$\frac{73\pi}{6} - \frac{72\pi}{6} = \frac{\pi}{46}$$

On the unit circle, the **y-coordinate** of any point is equal to the **sine** of the angle. At $\frac{\pi}{6}$ radians, the y–value is $\frac{1}{2}$.

Things to Remember:

- To simplify large angles in radians, subtract multiples of 2π until the angle is between 0 and 2π.
- On the unit circle, the sine of an angle corresponds to the y–coordinate.

135. Correct Answer: D. $\frac{20}{\cos\theta}$

To find an expression for the length of the hypotenuse AC in terms of angle θ, use the cosine ratio, which relates the adjacent side to the hypotenuse:

$$\cos\theta = \frac{adjacent}{hypotenuse}$$

$$\cos\theta = \frac{20}{AC}$$

To isolate AC, rearrange the equation by multiplying both sides by AC and then dividing by cosθ:

$\cos\theta = \frac{20}{AC}$	
$AC\cos\theta = 20$	Multiply
$AC = \frac{20}{\cos\theta}$	Divide

Things to Remember:

- Use SOH CAH TOA to remember trigonometric ratios: Sine = $\frac{Opposite}{hypotenuse}$, Cosine = $\frac{Adjacent}{hypotenuse}$ and Tangent = $\frac{Opposite}{Adjacent}$.

136. Correct Answer: 98

In triangle ABC, angle B is a right angle, angle C is 27°, and side BC (adjacent to angle C) is 14. First, calculate the length of leg AB (opposite to angle C) using the tangent ratio:

$$\tan(27°) = \frac{AB}{14}$$
$$AB = 14\tan(27°)$$

The area of a right triangle is calculated as Area = $\frac{1}{2}$ base × height. Use BC (14) as the base and AB (14tan(27°)) as the height:

$\text{Area} = \frac{1}{2} \text{ base} \times \text{height}$

$\text{Area} = \frac{1}{2} (14)14\tan(27°)$

$\text{Area} = 98\tan(27°)$

Comparing this result to the required form $k \tan(27°)$, we find that $k = 98$.

Things to Remember:

- The tangent of an angle in a right triangle is the ratio of the opposite leg to the adjacent leg.
- The area of a right triangle is $\frac{1}{2}$ base × height.

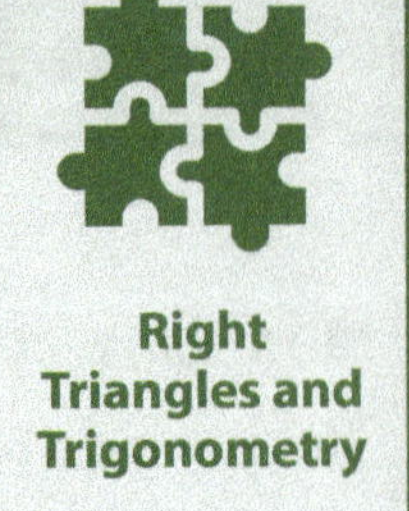

137. Correct Answer: A. $\frac{5\sqrt{6}}{13}$

The problem involves right triangle JKL, where angle J is the 90° right angle. We are given sin(K) and asked to find cos(L).

In any right triangle, the two non-right angles (K and L) are complementary, meaning they add to 90°. The **cofunction identity** states that the sine of an angle is equal to the cosine of its complement:

$$\sin(x) = \cos(90° - x)$$

$$\sin(K) = \cos(L)$$

Since the problem states that $\sin(K) = \frac{5\sqrt{6}}{13}$, the value of cos(L) must be identical, so $\cos(L) = \frac{5\sqrt{6}}{13}$.

Things to Remember:

- The sine of one acute angle in a right triangle is always equal to the cosine of the other acute angle.
- Complementary angles sum to 90° (or $\frac{\pi}{2}$ radians).

138. Correct Answer: 600

The questions asks for least possible horizontal distance x for a ramp that rises 30 inches, given the constraint $\tan\theta \leq \frac{1}{20}$. To solve, first define the angle theta based on the ramp's dimensions. In this right triangle, the rise (30) is the opposite side and the horizontal distance (*x*) is the adjacent side.

Set up the tangent expression to reflect this:

$$\tan\theta = \frac{\text{rise}}{\text{run}} = \frac{30}{x}$$

Relate this to the given constraint:

$$\tan\theta \leq \frac{1}{20}$$

$$\frac{30}{x} \leq \frac{1}{20}$$

Solve this expression to determine the least possible value of *x*:

$$\frac{30}{x} \leq \frac{1}{20}$$
$$600 \leq x$$

Things to Remember:

- Tangent represents the slope or "rise over run" of a line or ramp.

139 CIRCLES

Circle A in the xy–plane has the equation $(x - 1)^2 + (y + 4)^2 = 25$. Circle B has the same center as circle A, and the area of circle B is 4 times the area of circle A. The equation of circle B can be written as $(x - 1)^2 + (y + 4)^2 = k$, where k is a constant. What is the value of k?

140 CIRCLES

A circle in the xy–plane has a center at (– 2, 5). Line t is tangent to the circle at the point (6, b), where b is a constant. The slope of line t is $-\frac{3}{4}$. What is the value of b?

A. $\frac{41}{3}$

B. $\frac{47}{3}$

C. $\frac{49}{3}$

D. $\frac{53}{3}$

141 CIRCLES

A circle has center O. Points A and B lie on the circle. The measure of arc AB is 24°, and the length of arc AB is 6 inches. What is the circumference, in inches, of the circle?

A. 24

B. 60

C. 72

D. 90

142 CIRCLES

$$x^2 + y^2 + 8x - 12y - 28 = 0$$

In the xy–plane, the graph of the given equation is a circle. If this circle is inscribed in a square, what is the perimeter of the square?

A. $8\sqrt{5}$

B. $16\sqrt{5}$

C. $32\sqrt{5}$

D. $40\sqrt{5}$

GEOMETRY AND TRIGONOMETRY

143 CIRCLES

A circle is inscribed in a square so that the circle touches the midpoint of each side. The diagonal of the square is 196 units. What is the area, in square units, of the circle?

A. 2401π

B. 4802π

C. 9604π

D. 19208π

144 CIRCLES

A circle in the xy–plane has a center at (4, –1). A line t is tangent to the circle at the point (10, 2). What is the slope of line t?

A. $\frac{1}{2}$

B. $-\frac{1}{2}$

C. 2

D. –2

145 CIRCLES

Point A lies on the unit circle at (1, 0). The center O is located at (0, 0). Point B also lies on the unit circle, and the measure of angle AOB is radians. If the coordinates of point B are (a, b), what is the value of a?

A. $\frac{\sqrt{2}}{2}$

B. $-\frac{\sqrt{2}}{2}$

C. $-\frac{1}{2}$

D. $\frac{1}{2}$

146 CIRCLES

A circle has diameters PR and QS. The circumference of the circle is 96π. The length of arc RQ is three times the length of arc PQ. What is the length of arc RS?

A. 6π

B. 12π

C. 18π

D. 24π

CONTINUE

GEOMETRY AND TRIGONOMETRY

147 CIRCLES

The measure of angle P is $\frac{5\pi}{6}$ radians. The measure of angle Q is $\frac{7\pi}{12}$ radians greater than the measure of angle P. What is the measure of angle Q in degrees?

A. 195

B. 225

C. 255

D. 285

148 CIRCLES

$$x^2 + y^2 - 8x + 10y - 40 = 0$$

In the xy-plane, the graph of the equation is a circle. If this circle is inscribed in a square, what is the perimeter of the square?

A. 18

B. 36

C. 72

D. 144

149 CIRCLES

Point A lies on the unit circle at coordinates (0, 1). Point O is the center at (0, 0). Point B also lies on the circle and has coordinates $(x, -1)$, where x is a constant. Which of the following could be the positive measure of angle AOB, in radians?

A. $\frac{23\pi}{2}$

B. $\frac{25\pi}{2}$

C. 13π

D. $\frac{26\pi}{3}$

150 CIRCLES

A circle is drawn inside a square so that the circle touches the midpoint of each side of the square. The length of the square's diagonal is 140 units. What is the area, in square units, of the circle?

A. 2450π

B. 3650π

C. 4900π

D. 9800π

SEE SOLUTIONS ON NEXT PAGE

ANSWER KEY

QUESTIONS 139-150	
139	100
140	B
141	D
142	C
143	B
144	D
145	B
146	B
147	C
148	C
149	C
150	A

Don't just check the answer—master the method.
Get specific Desmos tips for each solution online. Gain access to The Gauntlet Mock Test and track your progress in real-time at **passthegauntlet.com.** Use code **GAUNTLETMATH20** to unlock 20% off your digital dashboard.

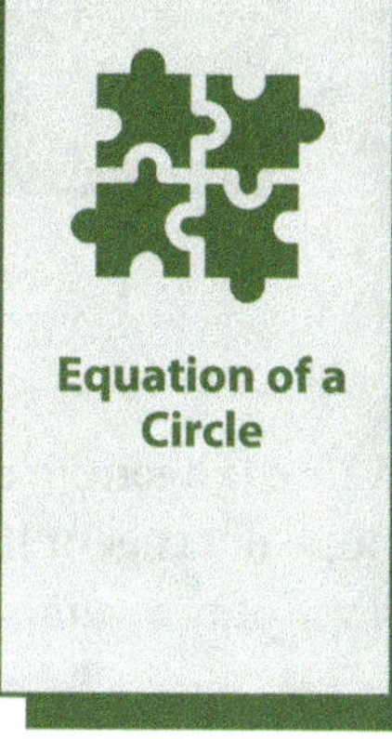

139. Correct Answer: 100

The goal is to find the value of k, which represents the r^2 of circle B. This can be found by evaluating the relationship between circle A and circle B. It is stated that the **area** of circle B is 4 times the area of circle A. When the area of a circle increases by a certain factor, the radius increases by the square root of that factor.

If the area of circle B is 4 times that of circle A, its radius is:

$$\sqrt{4} = 2 \text{ times as large}$$

From the equation of circle A, it can be determined that the radius of circle A is:

$$\sqrt{25} = 5$$

The radius of circle B is therefore:

$$5 \times 2 = 10$$

The value of k is equal to circle B's radius squared:

$$10^2 = 100$$

Things to Remember:

- The standard form of a circle equation is $(x - h)^2 + (y - k)^2 = r^2$, where (h, k) is the center and r is the radius.
- If the area of a circle is multiplied by n, the radius is multiplied by the square root of n.

Tangent Lines

140. Correct Answer: B. $\frac{47}{3}$

A line **tangent** to a circle is always **perpendicular** to the **radius** at the point of tangency. The given **slope** of **tangent line** t is $-\frac{3}{4}$. **Perpendicular lines** have **slopes** that are negative reciprocals, so the slope of the radius connecting the center (–2, 5) to the point (6, *b*) must be $\frac{4}{3}$.

Use the slope formula with the slope $\frac{4}{3}$, the center (–2, 5), and the point (6, *b*) to solve for *b*:

$$m = \frac{y_2 - y_1}{x_2 - x_1}$$

$\frac{4}{3} = \frac{b-5}{6-(-2)}$ Plug-in values

$\frac{4}{3} = \frac{b-5}{8}$ Simplify

$4(8) = 3(b-5)$ Cross-multiply

$32 = 3b - 15$ Distribute

$47 = 3b$ Add

$b = \frac{47}{3}$ Divide

Things to Remember:

- The radius to the point of tangency is always perpendicular to the tangent line.
- Perpendicular lines have slopes that are negative reciprocals of each other.

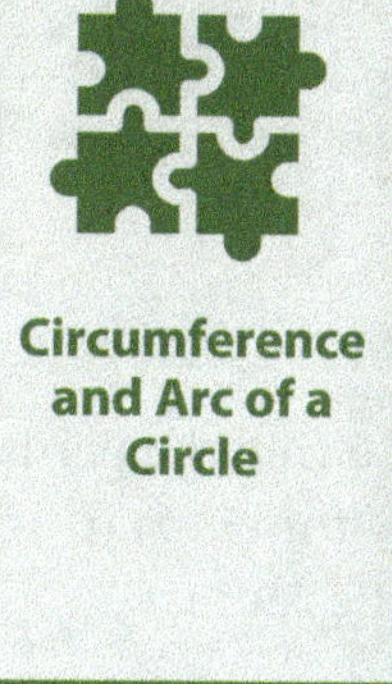

141. Correct Answer: D. 90

The arc length of a circle is proportional to its central angle. Use this relationship to determine the circumference of the circle:

$$\frac{\textit{arc length}}{\textit{circumference}} = \frac{\theta}{360}$$

$\frac{6}{x} = \frac{24}{360}$	Substitute
$24x = (360)(6)$	Cross-multiply
$24x = 2160$	Simplify
$x = 90$	Divide

Things to Remember:

- The ratio of arc length to circumference equals the ratio of the central angle to 360°.
- Use the proportion $\frac{\textit{arc length}}{\textit{circumference}} = \frac{\theta}{360}$ to solve for any unknown in arc length problems.

CONTINUE

Inscribed Circles

142. Correct Answer: C. $32\sqrt{5}$

To find the perimeter of the square, we must first determine the **diameter** of the circle inscribed within it. Start with the given equation $x^2 + y^2 + 8x - 12y - 28 = 0$ and **complete the square** to find the **radius:**

$$x^2 + y^2 + 8x - 12y - 28 = 0$$

$x^2 + y^2 + 8x - 12y = 28$	Add
$x^2 + 8x + y^2 - 12y = 28$	Rearrange
$(x^2 + 8x + 16) + (y^2 - 12y + 36) = 28 + 16 + 36$	Complete the square
$(x + 4)^2 + (y - 6)^2 = 80$	Factor

Since $r^2 = 80$, the radius r is the $\sqrt{80}$, which simplifies to $4\sqrt{5}$. The diameter is twice the radius:

$$d = 2(4\sqrt{5}) = 8\sqrt{5}$$

For a circle inscribed in a square, the diameter of the circle is equal to the side length of the square. Therefore, the perimeter is 4 times the side length:

$4(8\sqrt{5}) = 32\sqrt{5}$

Things to Remember:

- Completing the square allows you to find the radius and center from the general form of a circle equation.
- When a circle is inscribed in a square, the diameter of the circle equals the side length of the square.

SOLUTIONS
CIRCLES

143. Correct Answer: B. 4802π

A square's diagonal creates a **45 – 45 – 90 right triangle.** In this special triangle, the side length is the diagonal divided by the square root of 2.

$$\text{Side} = \frac{198}{\sqrt{2}} = \frac{98}{\sqrt{2}}$$

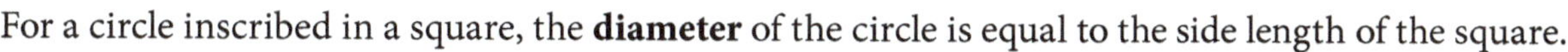

For a circle inscribed in a square, the **diameter** of the circle is equal to the side length of the square.

$$\text{Diameter} = 98\sqrt{2}$$

$$\text{Radius} = \frac{98}{\sqrt{2}} = 49\sqrt{2}$$

Use the **area** formula to find the final area of the circle:

$$\text{Area} = \pi r^2$$

$$\text{Area} = \pi(49\sqrt{2})^2$$

$$\text{Area} = \pi \times (2401 \times 2)$$

$$\textbf{Area} = \mathbf{4802\pi}$$

Things to Remember:

- For an inscribed circle, the diameter equals the side length of the square.
- The side of a square can be found by dividing the diagonal by the square root of 2.

SOLUTIONS
CIRCLES

144. Correct Answer: D. –2

To find the **slope** of **tangent line** *t*, we must first find the slope of the **radius** that connects to the point of tangency.

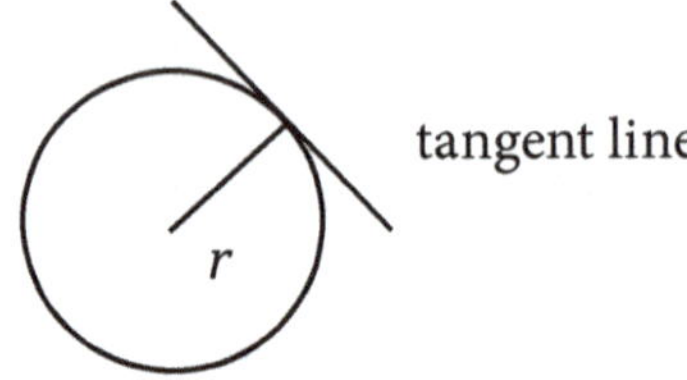

To find the slope of the **radius** use the **center** (4, –1) and the point (10, 2) with the **slope formula**.

$$\text{slope} = \frac{(y_2 - y_1)}{(x_2 - x_1)}$$

$$\text{slope} = \frac{2 - (-1)}{10 - 4}$$

$$\text{slope} = \frac{3}{6} = \frac{1}{2}$$

A line tangent to a circle is perpendicular to the radius at the point of tangency. Perpendicular lines have negative reciprocal slopes. The negative reciprocal of $\frac{1}{2}$ is –2.

Therefore, the answer is –2.

Things to Remember:

- Tangent lines are always perpendicular to the radius at the point of tangency.
- Perpendicular lines have slopes that are negative reciprocals.

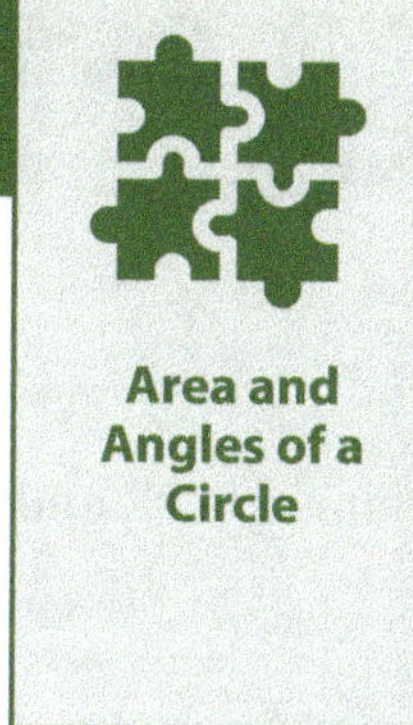

145. Correct Answer: B. $\frac{-\sqrt{2}}{2}$

To find the **x–coordinate** of point B on the **unit circle** given an angle of $\frac{395\pi}{4}$ radians, the angle must be simplified to a **coterminal angle** between 0 and 2π by removing full rotations.

One full rotation is 2π, so find a multiple of 2π that is closest to $\frac{395\pi}{4}$.

$$2\pi = \frac{8\pi}{4}$$

$$\frac{8\pi}{4} \times 49 = \frac{392\pi}{4}$$

Subtract $\frac{392\pi}{4}$ from $\frac{395\pi}{4}$ to determine the remaining angle left over:

$$\frac{395\pi}{4} - \frac{392\pi}{4} = \frac{3\pi}{4}$$

On the unit circle, the **x-coordinate** of any point is equal to the **cosine** of the angle. At $\frac{3\pi}{4}$ radians (which is 135 degrees), the x-value is $\frac{-\sqrt{2}}{2}$.

Things to Remember:

- On a unit circle, the coordinates are ($\cos\theta$, $\sin\theta$).
- Subtract multiples of 2π to find simplified coterminal angles.

SOLUTIONS
CIRCLES

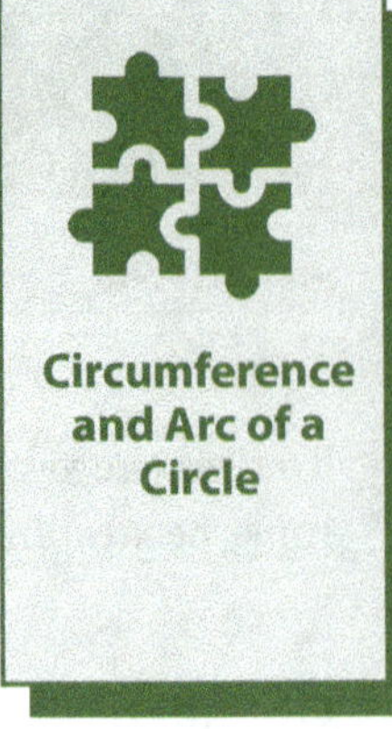

146. Correct Answer: B. 12π

Diameters PR and QS divide the circle into four arcs. Vertical arcs are equal, so:

$$\text{arc } PQ = \text{arc } RS$$

$$\text{arc } RQ = \text{arc } SP$$

Let arc PQ = x. The problem states arc RQ is three times the length of arc PQ, so:

$$\text{arc } RQ = 3x$$

Since vertical arcs are equal, the total circumference is:

$$PQ + RQ + RS + SP = x + 3x + x + 3x = 8x$$

We are given the circumference is 96π.

$$8x = 96\pi$$

$$x = 12\pi$$

Since arc RS is equal to x, its length is 12π.

Things to Remember:

- Intersecting diameters create equal vertical arcs.
- The sum of all arcs in a circle equals its total circumference.

Circumference and Arc of a Circle

147. Correct Answer: C. 255

To find the measure of angle Q in degrees, start by first determining the **radian** value of angle Q. The problem states angle Q is $\frac{7\pi}{12}$ radians greater than angle P which is $\frac{5\pi}{6}$.

$Q = \frac{7\pi}{12} + \frac{5\pi}{6}$
$Q = \frac{7\pi}{12} + \frac{10\pi}{12}$
$Q = \frac{17\pi}{12}$

To convert **radians** to **degrees**, multiply the **radian** measure by $\frac{180}{\pi}$.

$$\frac{17\pi}{12} \times \frac{180}{\pi} = 17 * 15 = 255$$

Things to Remember:

- To convert **radians** to **degrees**, multiply by $\frac{180}{\pi}$.
- When adding fractions with π, find a common denominator before combining them.

SOLUTIONS
CIRCLES

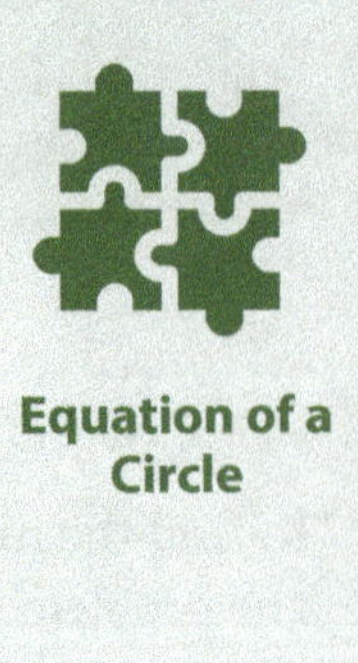

148. Correct Answer: C. 72

To find the perimeter of the square, you must first determine the **radius** and **diameter** of the circle inscribed within it. Complete the square to find the **radius:**

$x^2 + y^2 - 8x + 10y - 40 = 0$

$x^2 + y^2 - 8x + 10y = 40$ Add 40

$(x^2 - 8x) + (y^2 + 10y) = 40$ Group terms

$(x^2 - 8x + 16) + (y^2 + 10y + 25) = 40 + 16 + 25$ Complete the square

$(x - 4)^2 + (y + 5)^2 = 81$ Factor and simplify

The **radius** squared (r^2) is 81, so the **radius** $r = 9$. The **diameter** (d) is twice the radius:

$$d = 2 \times 9$$

$$d = 18$$

Since the circle is inscribed in a square, the **diameter** is equal to the **side length** of the square. Use this to determine the perimeter of the square.

$$\text{Perimeter} = 4s$$

$$\text{P} = 4 \times 18$$

$$\text{P} = 72$$

Things to Remember:

- The standard form of a circle equation is $(x - h)^2 + (y - k)^2 = r^2$, where r is the radius.
- For an inscribed circle, the diameter of the circle is equal to the side length of the square.

149. Correct Answer: C. 13π

This question involves using the **unit circle** to evaluate the measure of an angle. Start by finding the missing x–coordinate of Point B by substituting $y = -1$ into the **unit circle** equation:

$x^2 + y^2 = 1$	Unit circle equation
$x^2 + (-1)^2 = 1$	Substitute
$x^2 + 1 = 1$	Simplify exponent
$x^2 = 0$	Subtract
$x = 0$	Take the square root

The coordinates of Point B are $(0, -1)$. Use this to identify the angles:

- Point A is at (0, 1), which corresponds to $\frac{\pi}{2}$ radians on the unit circle.
- Point B is at (0, –1), which corresponds to $\frac{3\pi}{2}$ radians on the unit circle.

Calculate the angle difference:

$$\text{Angle AOB} = \frac{3\pi}{2} - \frac{\pi}{2} = \pi$$

Angle AOB can be any odd integer multiple of π. The only answer that satisfies this requirement is 13π.

Things to Remember:

- The unit circle has a radius of 1 and is centered at (0, 0).
- Angle measures are periodic so adding multiples of 2π creates coterminal angles.

CONTINUE

150. Correct Answer: A. 2450π

This problem requires finding the **area of a circle** based on the **diagonal** of the square it is inscribed in. Drawing out the problem will help you with understanding how to solve.

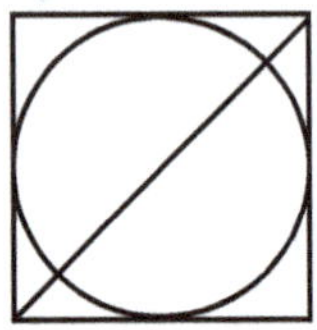

Use the given **diagonal** to find the side length of the square. The **diagonal** of a square creates two 45:45:90 triangles with side ratios of x:x:$x\sqrt{2}$.

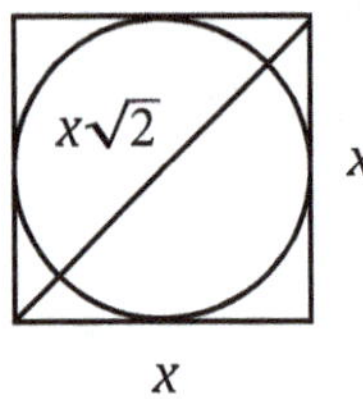

Therefore, the side length of the square is equal to the **diagonal** divided by the square root of 2.

$$x = \frac{140}{\sqrt{2}}$$

$$x = \frac{70}{\sqrt{2}}$$

Since the circle touches the midpoints of the square's sides, its **diameter** is equal to the square's side length. Since the **radius** is equal to half the **diameter**, divide the **diameter** of $70\sqrt{2}$ by 2:

$$\frac{70\sqrt{2}}{2} = 35\sqrt{2}$$

Use the area formula to calculate the **area of the circle**:

$$A = \pi r^2$$

$$A = \pi(35\sqrt{2})^2$$

$$A = 2450\pi$$

Things to Remember:

- 45:45:90 triangles have side ratios of x:x:$x\sqrt{2}$.
- The area of a circle is calculated using the formula $A = \pi r^2$.

ABOUT THE AUTHORS

John McDowell

John McDowell is the founder of Mr. John's Test Prep and the creator of *The Gauntlet* series. A premier test prep architect with over a decade of experience, John has dedicated thousands of hours to helping students overcome the psychological and analytical hurdles of the SAT. Based in Bradenton, Florida, and a prominent member of the National Test Prep Association, he is recognized for his "no-nonsense" approach to achieving elite scores.

John holds an MA in Applied Linguistics from Georgia State University, a background that deeply informs his data-driven methods for language acquisition and test logic. He currently serves as a full-time teacher at a private high school's Learning Resource Center, where he specializes in executive function coaching. This dual expertise in linguistics and cognitive strategy has allowed him to mentor numerous students to perfect 800 scores in both the Math and Verbal sections of the SAT.

When he isn't refining the strategies that power *The Gauntlet* or mentoring students across the country, John can usually be found out on the water fishing or helping his wife manage the logistics of her local sourdough bakery business.

Cierra Henderson

Cierra Henderson is an experienced educator based out of Massachusetts who has tutored students across all grade levels and subjects, with a specialization in SAT and test preparation as well as executive functioning support. Her background includes tutoring in math, science, English, and history, along with standardized exams such as the SAT, ACT, ISEE, and SSAT.

She holds a certificate in educational consulting from the University of California Irvine, and supports students through the college application process, from selecting colleges to essay development and final submission. Cierra's tutoring approach emphasizes individualized instruction, purposeful practice, and strategic skill building, delivered through a compassionate, student-centered learning experience.

www.ingramcontent.com/pod-product-compliance
Lightning Source LLC
LaVergne TN
LVHW061202120826
845149LV00011B/1882

* 9 7 9 8 9 9 5 0 7 0 7 2 6 *